TWENTY

GUYS

YOU DATE

IN YOUR

TWENTIES

TWENTY

GUYS

YOU DATE

IN YOUR

TWENTIES

GABI CONTI

CHRONICLE BOOKS

San Francisco

Library of Congress Cataloging-in-Publication Data:

Names: Conti, Gabi, author.
Title: 20 guys you date in your 20s / Gabi Conti.
Other titles: Twenty guys you date in your twenties
Description: San Francisco : Chronicle Books, [2020]
Identifiers: LCCN 2019018728 | ISBN 9781452179742 (pbk. : alk. paper)
Subjects: LCSH: Dating (Social customs) | Man-woman relationships.
Classification: LCC HQ801.A512 C57 2020 | DDC 306.73—dc23
LC record available at https://lccn.loc.gov/2019018728

Manufactured in China.

Design and Illustration by Rachel Harrell.

Collage art by Leah Peugh.

10 9 8 7 6 5 4 3 2 1

Chronicle books and gifts are available at special quantity discounts to
corporations, professional associations, literacy programs, and other
organizations. For details and discount information, please contact our
premiums department at corporatesales@chroniclebooks.com or at
1-800-759-0190.

Chronicle Books LLC
680 Second Street
San Francisco, California 94107
www.chroniclebooks.com

TABLE OF CONTENTS

DEDICATION

This book is dedicated to my parents, Julie and Paul Conti, who remind me what a healthy relationship looks like through their forty years of marriage. No matter how many times my heart gets broken, my parents make me believe true love is possible.

And to the twenty guys I dated in my twenties: Thank you. Next.

PREFACE

Names and identifying details have been changed to protect the privacy of individuals and the very fragile male ego.

All ages in the book reflect when this manuscript was first written in 2019.

NEW BOOK, WHO DIS?

I'm a hopeless romantic who has always had terrible luck with dating. I'm kind of like Taylor Swift, but with less of a girl squad and more of a belly button. So, I started talking about it. At first with my girlfriends over brunch, then (per their request) with a licensed therapist. I also went on a lot of dates. Since I was single for most of my twenties, I dated about two guys a year, with many first and last dates in between.

Then I did the math. Wow. I easily went on ten thousand hours' worth of dates in my twenties. According to Malcolm Gladwell, that makes me an expert. A dating expert. The more I dated, the more I wrote, and eventually, I turned my experiences into a book. At the time, every pitch I sent to the female-driven blogs I contributed to gave me the very helpful feedback of, "Love it! But can you make it a list?!" So I did, and *Twenty Guys You Date in Your Twenties* was born.

I soon realized there are timeless tropes, or patterns, in dating and relationships. Remember when ghosting became a thing, and everyone was like, "That happened to me!"? Well, there's plenty more where that came from. Twenty in fact! Yep, there are about twenty different types of guys you will date in your twenties.

But this book isn't meant to be man-shaming. A lot of these types go both ways. Just because you're dating a type of guy in the book doesn't mean you should dump him immediately! We all have our issues. There are even tools in here to show you how to make it work.

Your twenties can also be a state of mind. A time when anything feels uncertain or new. Maybe you are just getting out of a long-term relationship or marriage and haven't been single since high school. I got you. Dating in your twenties can be full of obstacles, like roommates, distance, or that little voice in your head that keeps screaming, "What are you doing with your life?!" To quote Ally McBeal, "Love is, um, well, it's like an obstacle course and some people let the obstacles win, and then there are those who don't."

This book is for those who don't let the obstacles of dating in your twenties win. You may even discover that the guy who becomes your person is one (or more) of these guys. Which is totally fine! Just because your guy fits into this or that category doesn't mean your relationship won't work. Each chapter of this book is meant to help you navigate your way through the zoo that is dating in your twenties. You know, that fun and flirty time when it feels like everyone else around you is pairing off Noah's Ark style, and you're stranded in the wild just trying to get a text back?

Well, that basically makes you a unicorn, and unicorns are, like, *really* pretty. So you're, like, *really* pretty! Beyond the challenge of dating in your twenties, dating at any age today can feel impossible. While social media is bringing us together, it's also tearing us apart. There's the white noise of rom-coms, reality dating shows, and love songs. *The Bachelor* convinces us that it's normal to propose to someone you've known for only nine weeks. It's not. That's why only one out of the twenty-two *Bachelor* winning couples are still together. That's a 4.5 percent success rate! Disney raised us to believe that if we're patient and kind to animals, and fall asleep at just the right time, someday our prince will come. But when he finally does come, all you get from his magic carpet ride is a raging UTI.

This book features short stories about my dating failures and successes. While dating can be terrible, it can also be funny (after enough time has passed). All of my dates have been given aliases to protect their privacy and to protect me from a flood of angry emails/lawsuits. I've given each guy a chance to approve and weigh in on his story. As a journalist, I know you have to fact-check! This book is also filled with fun graphics, charts, and quizzes, along with advice from successful couples who overcame their obstacles, dating experts, and even the guys I dated. Love is a battlefield: Use this book as a shield—or a sword, if that's your style.

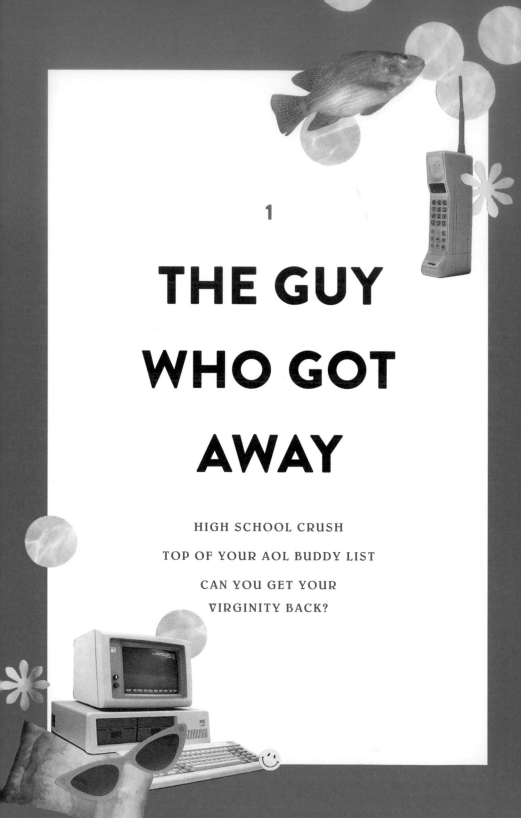

1

THE GUY WHO GOT AWAY

HIGH SCHOOL CRUSH
TOP OF YOUR AOL BUDDY LIST
CAN YOU GET YOUR
VIRGINITY BACK?

"tell me everything," Vincent gushed, slurping a noodle at the only Thai restaurant in Westport, Connecticut. I was 16 and had just lost my virginity to my boyfriend, Will.

The week before, Will handed me a condom and said gently, "Whenever you're ready, you can give me this, and I'll know." So obviously the first person I went to was my gay best friend, Vincent. We rehearsed how I would hand Will the condom. I had to be coy but also seductive.

"I blew the condom thing," I admitted.

"I bet that's not the only thing you blew," Vincent smirked.

I told Vincent how I walked into Will's house (his parents were out of town), threw the condom at him, and exclaimed, "I am ready. Let's do this!" with the gusto of a 52-year-old divorcée. Vincent facepalmed. Then we toasted our Thai iced teas to me finally becoming a woman. Honestly, gossiping over chicken pad thai with my best friend was my favorite part of losing my virginity.

Will and I came from different worlds. My world was musical theater with Vincent. We lived and breathed high school theater, despite never getting any leads. We were convinced it was because we were just too fabulous! Vincent and I were outcasts in the theater department because we liked to party, but the popular kids thought we were weird because we did theater. Will always seemed to be surrounded by friends in the cafeteria no matter what time of day it was. But somehow, he was a good student. He was a senior, on the swim team, and 420 friendly.

Despite our differences, Will and I bonded online, even though my screen name was DramaQueenGC. It began when Will, or Wlbrt86, IMed me "Sup" one afternoon. So I tried out a new away message: "Shower. Care to join me? ;)"

I realize now this sounds like the flirting tactics of a cougar. But my suggestive status worked. Wlbrt86 asked me out on Christmas Eve. He picked me up in his silver Nissan, and we drove to the beach. We listened to the Black Eyed Peas, the good stuff where Fergie was less featured. He looked deep into my eyes, our faces glowed from his dashboard lights, and . . . he kissed me. My heart raced.

Soon I got to know Will, instead of Wlbrt86. He was funny and a good friend, with this mole on his cheek I found incredibly sexy because I was really into

TASTE:	LOOK:	SOUND:	SMELL:	FEEL:
Watermelon Smirnoff vodka	Popped collar, puka shell necklace, and strategically spiked hair	"The One Who Got Away" (Acoustic) by Katy Perry	Cafeteria french fries frying	Like the luckiest girl in high school

Enrique Iglesias at the time. After we had sex, things got serious. We went to his prom and were inseparable the entire summer. I really thought this relationship would last. But we broke up when he went to college. After that, he always had a girlfriend, but deep down I wondered if someday we'd end up together.

We lost touch until I was 28 and visiting New York over the holidays. I invited him to my comedy show, because if there's one surefire way to impress the guy you lost your virginity to, it's with a two-drink minimum and dick jokes.

After the show, we caught up. I don't know if it was the Christmas spirit, the vodka sodas, or how we joked it would've been the twelfth anniversary of our first date, but when Will kissed me, I felt my heart race all over again, like I was in the front seat of his silver Nissan on Christmas Eve 2003.

I wondered if maybe this time it would work. Maybe I spent all these hours dating only to end up where I began. Deep down, I kind of hoped so. Until I realized we were from different worlds now. The only thing we had in common was being in love once. If we tried to date again, it would be like forcing an old AOL CD-ROM into a MacBook Air.

I didn't talk to Will again until I was writing this. I knew he had a girlfriend. So I Facebook-messaged him to be less invasive. I didn't get a response. The next morning I opened up Instagram and saw a picture of him, his girlfriend, and a shiny ring. I imagined him, ring in pocket, and my message buzzing. I guess some things are meant to stay in the past. Sometimes The Guy Who Got Away got away for a reason. And while it might be hard to accept, you just have to listen to AOL and say, "Goodbye."

BOY BINGO

Dated/crushed on him in high school	Are no longer in each other's lives	Your first love
Lost your virginity to him	**Free space!**	**Been unavailable since you broke up**

Don't live near each other	**Still wonder, _what if?_**	**Used to be your best friend**

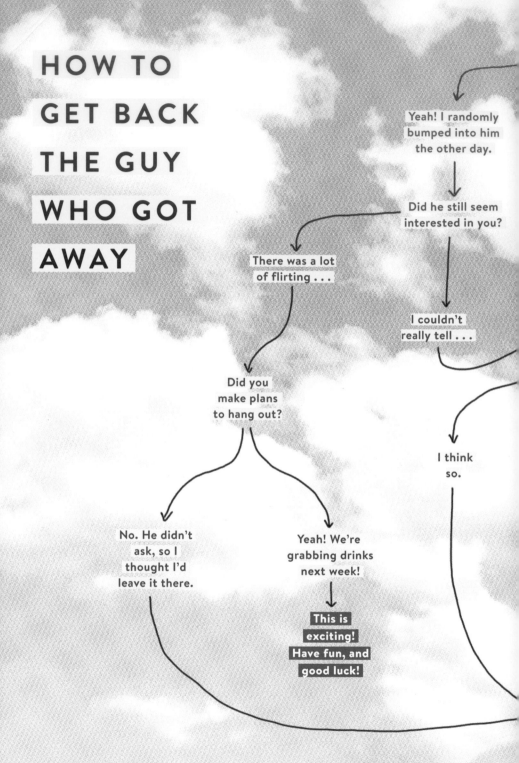

HOW TO GET BACK THE GUY WHO GOT AWAY

Yeah! I randomly bumped into him the other day.

Did he still seem interested in you?

There was a lot of flirting . . .

I couldn't really tell . . .

Did you make plans to hang out?

I think so.

No. He didn't ask, so I thought I'd leave it there.

Yeah! We're grabbing drinks next week!

This is exciting! Have fun, and good luck!

HAVE YOU TALKED SINCE HIGH SCHOOL?

Not really.

Does he live close to you?

He does!

No :(

Will you ever be in the same zip code?

Is he in a relationship?

Yeah! Over the holidays!

Not likely.

Doesn't look like it.

And he's single?

Is he seeing anyone?

Yeah!

No.

Doesn't look like it.

Ask him to grab a drink to catch up!

Let him go. If he returns (single), ask him out. If he doesn't, set him free.

Yeah . . .

Try talking again. Who knows what the future holds?

How to Ignite an Old Flame

Do an online search.

Try all forms of social media, including LinkedIn. (I had good luck with LinkedIn when I was reaching out to exes for this book. It feels the most professional and least invasive, which could be good if he's seeing someone.) Follow and/or direct-message him on the platform of your choice.

Connect with mutual friends.

Find out if he stays in touch with them. Try to see if he ever mentions you, or what they think he might feel about reuniting with you.

Call his mom!

She liked you, right? Use something like Mother's Day, Valentine's Day, or any holiday, really, to give her a call to catch up. Casually mention the Guy Who Got Away, but don't make him the main focus of the conversation.

Have a drink at his favorite bar.

You know the spot. The haunt you haven't gone to since you broke up. Sit at the bar when it's slow and chat with the bartender. Find out if The Guy Who Got Away is still a regular and who he's regularly been drinking with.

Connect with his ex.

You know, the one he dated before or after you. Now that you're both not dating him, you have something in common! Worst case, you make a new girlfriend!

Ask Someone Else

Guy I Dated: Will, 32, dated for 9 months in high school, and 1 date in 2016

I love the story. My only advice is to try to live in the moment without regrets. Whether it ends up working out the way you hoped or not, what's important is enjoying it while it's happening. It helps shape your perception of relationships and who you are, so embrace it all. Also, regarding the whole condom thing, at that moment, I probably thought it was such a smooth move. Looking back, I cringe a little and realize I wasn't quite the Romeo I thought I was. Sorry, you can't get your virginity back!

Couple: JoAnn, 52, & Steve, 55, together 7 years

We met in college. I was a junior and she was a freshman. I graduated and never thought about her. I ran into her a few years later, but nothing happened. Then, in 2011, we reconnected through work and started friendly emailing. I finally asked for her number, and we started texting. I eventually called her one night, and we talked for over three hours. The next time we chatted I asked her if I could fly her to LA, which she accepted. We had a blast, and for the next almost two years, I flew back every month to see her for a week or flew her out to see me. One day we decided she should move to LA. Now, we're engaged and live in New Jersey. My advice is to never think you won't meet anyone. JoAnn was never married and met me when she was 45. I was divorced for over ten years and never ever thought I would fall for somebody across the country. Also, always make sure a guy treats you right and isn't a phony. Sure, bad boys are "cool" but there is a reason they are called bad boys.

Expert: David Feliciano, former detective sergeant, Westchester County Sheriff's Office, Fugitive Unit

When I was looking for fugitives, I used to contact alumni associations like high schools, colleges, etc. They always have info on people, and someone is always organizing a reunion. Mailmen also know more about people than anyone realizes. After all, they read your mail when bored. Check out their old hangouts, buddies, etc. Some of the best sources are brothers, sisters, and bartenders. Look into professional associations like clubs, fraternities, etc. Look into pissed off old girlfriends or ex-wives. Old bosses, too. Just say you are doing a background check for a headhunter agency. Moms are also good sources if they liked you. If he drives an expensive car, look into car clubs, like Corvette or Porsche. If he's religious, contact his place of worship. I once tracked down a guy who put a stone on his mother's grave on the anniversary of her passing. I was there all day, but I got my man. When I'd contact these people, I'd usually say I was looking for them because they won a raffle, lottery, or trip. Wait, you're not trying to stalk this guy, are you?

2

THE GUY WHO'S HOTTER THAN YOU

MODEL?

LIVES FOR SELFIES

"LOVE" AT
FIRST SIGHT

1 t was freshman orientation. I was supposed to be watching Emerson College's president give a speech about . . . I don't know. I wasn't there. I was at Hudson's apartment. He was a super senior. We had been dating for only eight days, but I was already smitten. I liked everything about him, from how he shook his shaggy, dark hair away from his thick eyebrows, to the tiny gap between his teeth. I was impressed by how his North End apartment had an exposed brick wall (on purpose) and art that hung in actual frames! Sure, he had a roommate, but get this: They had their own rooms!

He grabbed jeans off the floor and slipped them on. They were my jeans. Not only did my boot cut denim fit him, but he looked better in them than I did. Which made sense. Hudson was a model. I mean, *of course* he was a model. His name was *Hudson*. While I never saw any of his work, the night we met he told me about his runway and print experience. I believed him since he was tall and had a lot of product in his hair, which I assumed was from a shoot. I told him I also worked in the fashion industry. Sure, I folded jeans at a trendy women's retail store, but one on Newbury Street, which duck boat tour guides called, "the Rodeo drive of Boston," so, same?

"Can you get me these in the biggest size they have?" he asked, knowing they came from the store I worked at.

"For sure! I can use my employee discount!" *Please like me*, I thought.

"Actually do these come in any other colors?"

"Uh, red corduroy . . . "

His face lit up. "Oh yes! Those would go great with my Uggs! Thanks, babe." He kissed me on the cheek. I smiled, ignoring this big red corduroy flag that the guy I was dating wanted me to buy him a pair of red velvety *women's* pants to wear with his *Ugg* boots. I was too distracted by the fact that he just called me "Babe," which I was pretty sure made us official? We hadn't defined our relationship yet, but this felt promising!

I met Hudson the week prior outside my dorm building. I was smoking a clove cigarette, which I kept in a "vintage" (Urban Outfitters) aluminum case. Hudson approached me and my freshman friends with a group of upperclassmen who looked like Vampire Weekend sounds. He invited us

TASTE:	LOOK:	SOUND:	SMELL:	FEEL:
Coconut and pineapple. Wait. Did he get a spray tan?	Like he's always walking in slow motion	The synthesizer of runway music	The beach. You're nowhere near a beach.	So soft. Seriously though, how does he get his skin that smooth?

to a party off campus. My mind said no, but my clove cigarette said yes.

That night we had our first kiss, under string lights and stars, as Little Italy's aroma of cannoli frying, garlic, and the start of autumn filled the air. From that kiss, we dated in fast-forward. He made me a mix CD and cooked me salmon for dinner. (Just salmon. Again, male model.)

So the least I could do was get him those corduroys! The next day after work, I could buy anything with my employee discount, but it had to be for me. I grabbed the corduroys, palms sweating. My manager rang me up, questioning why I was buying a size 32 when she knew I was a 26. I blamed it on the freshman fifteen (classes hadn't even started yet). She sympathized, suggested I chew gum the next time I was hungry, and rang me up.

Hudson loved his corduroys. "Gabi scored these for me!" he'd brag to people, kissing me on the cheek. So this basically made him my boyfriend, right?

Wrong. Turns out he was dating someone else. Despite his fashion choices, that someone else was a girl. I was heartbroken. I played Green Day's "Wake Me Up When September Ends" on loop. It was only September 3. I would've kept listening to it way past the end of September, but my roommate begged me to stop. I couldn't believe that if a guy cooked you salmon and made you a mix CD, and you bought him red corduroys, that didn't automatically make him your boyfriend.

And then it hit me. Who was this person smoking clove cigarettes and listening to sad music? This wasn't me. I was so consumed with dating someone "better looking" than me that I started changing *my* look. College is all about finding yourself, but that doesn't mean changing who you are.

How to Look Hot When Your Date Is Hotter than You

Important: Read all of the steps before attempting.

Step 1:

Take a long shower. Shave off all your body hair while wearing a deep conditioning hair mask.

Step 2:

Lay on your bed in a towel and stare at the ceiling for at least twenty minutes. Set an intention for how you can be hotter.

Step 3:

Apply a sheet mask and eye patches while you do 14–22 sit-ups, followed by holding a plank for a minute.

Step 4:

Time for makeup! Perfect smile! Do a full face contour. Apply fake lashes and a shadow that makes your eyes pop!

Step 5:

Apply clip-on hair extensions and perfectly curl your "hair" until you look like a Victoria's Secret Angel.

Step 6:

Try on everything in your closet. Cry because you have nothing to wear. Drink a glass of wine. Settle on your little black dress.

Step 7:

Disregard Steps 1–6. Because stop it. You're already hot!

BOY BINGO

Can pull off white after Labor Day	**Most of his pictures are of himself and professionally taken**	**Takes longer to get ready than you**
Often gets mistaken for a celebrity	**Free space!** 	**Face products are more expensive than yours**
Can get a bartender's attention faster than you	**You both require the same amount of grooming products**	**"Love" at first sight**

Quiz

WHAT KIND OF HOT GUY ARE YOU DATING?

When you tell him he's hot, what does he do?

(A) Says, "I know," as he admires his reflection in the window behind you.

(B) Blushes and says, "I am not!" and gets really uncomfortable.

(C) Reminds you that our planet is actually what's getting hotter, and we need to do something about global warming!

What's his morning routine like?

(A) Long and tedious. Almost a play-by-play of Patrick Bateman's in *American Psycho.*

(B) Simple. Less of a routine and more getting out of the door.

(C) Rolls out of bed, ready to roll onto a runway.

How long has he been hot?

How many pictures does he post of himself?

A All his life. Please stop asking him questions about it. He knows he's good looking. He also knows he looks just like that actor/musician/model/reality star.

B He really doesn't think he's hot! He used to be awkward as a kid and hasn't accepted his good looks yet.

C He really doesn't think about his looks that much. He's more concerned about our political climate, TBH.

A A lot. But it's, like, his job. He really wishes he didn't have to.

B Oh god. None! He hates having his picture taken and never knows what to do with his hands! Please, don't take his picture!

C None.

Who spends more money on clothes?

A Him, but he's pretty sure it's a tax write-off since it's an investment in his modeling career.

B You. He's never been shopping unless it's with his mom.

C You. All his clothes are secondhand to reduce his carbon footprint.

Mostly Ⓐ

Male Model: Whether professional or not, this guy is very consumed by his looks. As long as you stay confident, respect each other, and don't get jealous, this could work out!

Mostly Ⓑ

Sexy, and He Doesn't Know It: He's the most beautiful boy (in the room). He's either been fat or geeky or both, and is unaware or uncomfortable with his blossoming good looks. Enjoy it before it goes to his head.

Mostly Ⓒ

Woke Up Like This: Has no desire to be a model, but easily could be. People have been telling him since birth that he's good looking, and honestly, he's over it. There's so much he wants to do in this life. Getting paid to be hot just isn't one of them!

Signs This
Guy Is Too Hot
to Be True

———

No, he definitely did not wake up like that.

Hair:
Involves a lot of product
and at least 30 minutes of
undivided attention.

Eyebrows:
He gets these waxed
or threaded.

Face:
Tinted SPF moisturizer.
No, it is not makeup, and
no, you cannot borrow it.
It's Armani!

Eyes:
Shh, these are color
contacts. Don't tell his
modeling agent.

Glasses:
These are fake.

V-Neck:
Lower and more
expensive than yours.

Sneakers:
He'll never admit it, but
he waited in line for
3 hours just to snag these.
Sick, right?

Chest:
He shaves this.

Skin:
That's a spray tan.

Jeans:
Tighter, smaller, and more
expensive than yours.

Bag:
It's not a man purse!
It's a gender-neutral bag,
and he needs it! He has
a lot of stuff! (Mostly
condoms.)

Ask Someone Else

Guy I Dated: Hudson, 35, dated for 1 month

Aw, this is great and certainly a hell of a lot nicer than it could have been. It's so funny and brings back so many memories. Vampire Weekend, lol. I'm sorry I don't have the red corduroys, due in fact to a very real and very unfortunate post-college fifteen, but I do still cherish them. :)

Couple: Sammie, 31, & Tom, 32, together 12 years

Since my husband, Tom, and I moved to France, he seems to have found his best Euro self. He walks way more, grew out his hair, and updated his wardrobe (Paris does that to you). I have stayed the same. I always found him attractive, but he has definitely gone up a notch. Multiple friends have noticed, and even Tom knows he has gotten better looking (but he's very humble and would never say it). He will tell me after a workout class that he noticed people checking him out. I think

it's fantastic. And yes, I think he is 100 percent more attractive than me. And you want to know how that makes me feel? Like one lucky girl. He thinks I'm nuts for saying it. It's okay. I'm cool with it. I'm very confident in our relationship. I am also confident he likes the way I look. You really need to love yourself, even if the person isn't more attractive. You can't be in a healthy relationship with another human until you are in a healthy relationship with yourself. When you love yourself, you know you are deserving of the person who loves you, whether you think they are more attractive than you or not. Be grateful when someone you happen to be married to just happens to improve with age.

Expert: Chris James, 49, former international fashion model, current national touring comedian

I would see if he introduces you to very close friends or family and inner social circles. That will determine

how into you he is. Guys in their twenties are not that mature and tend to be easily tempted by women at parties and social events. I was pretty steady with one woman in particular, and she was not industry-standard hot. But she was healthy, funny, and just a joy to be around. She would poke fun at the pretentiousness of the surroundings and was not insecure about her looks. That made her way more attractive to me. She was quick and funny in her interactions with people. My advice is to act like you are hot without being cocky, and men will find that attractive.

3

THE GUY WHO'S LONG DISTANCE

HE'S SO BUSY!

THE PEN PAL

DOES HE EXIST?

growing up my favorite song was "Hopelessly Devoted to You," from the movie *Grease*. Sure, I was six, and there wasn't anything close to a "you" in my life. But I couldn't wait to someday have a "you." Love sounded amazing—to be devoted to someone so hopelessly that there aren't any words left, just song. Sign me up!

Music didn't play a role in my love life until the summer I went back to my camp as a counselor. There I met James. He was also an adult counselor. He had this manicured, rugged look, like he could take care of me in an apocalypse, but not in a gross, roughing it kind of way.

We met in the dining hall by the coffee dispenser. Apparently, we were the only two people at this all-girls summer camp in Maine who needed caffeine to properly function in the morning—which made sense since 80 percent of the camp was either a child or Mormon.

One night after work, we bumped into each other by the jukebox at a dive bar. I was on a mission to play Bob Dylan's "Stuck Inside of Mobile with the Memphis Blues Again," because I

was attending a liberal arts college and wanted everyone to know it, and he was determined to play something by Bruce Springsteen, despite not being from New Jersey. We talked about our favorite songs. Watching him light up about the bands he liked made me instantly fall for James. I was so over the Australian tennis instructor I had been dating the previous week, whose favorite song was "Land Down Under," as if the accent he laid on as thick as his body spray wasn't obvious enough.

Later that night my new Summer Boyfriend (who I was dating only in my head) and I went for a moonlight swim in the lake. There we had our first kiss. This might sound romantic, but have your feet ever touched the floor of a lake? It's slimy and unknown. Also, it's very difficult to make out and tread water at the same time, and I'm a decent swimmer.

The next morning at the coffee dispenser, James handed me a Modest Mouse CD. I listened to it every night while falling asleep. This was the first track to my love soundtrack with a guy whose middle name I didn't know yet.

TASTE:	LOOK:	SOUND:	SMELL:	FEEL:
Airplane nuts	Those 3–5 photos you show friends of the guy you're "kind of sort of seeing"	That one song . . . your song. (He has no clue you have a song.)	The fuel of a jet plane mixed with the aroma of Auntie Anne's pretzels	Hopeful exciting butterflies mixed with a sinking sadness when you realize it's going to be a while until you see each other again

When summer ended, I gave back the CD with my number inside.

He never called, but he wrote on my Facebook wall asking if I'd heard this new Bob Dylan cover album. This began a back-and-forth, three-year Facebook wall post-ship where we would suggest music to one other and then critique those albums on each other's walls. Then we started sending CDs.

His music taste was hard to match, especially because of my facade that I lived for alternative rock. In reality, my music preference could best be described as, "John Mayer meets show tunes!" To keep up, I'd track the charts and read album reviews. This was pre-Spotify, so it was basically a part-time job.

Valentine's Day of my senior year, James made a trip to visit me in Boston. We got into our first fight about destiny. I believed there was a reason we met and kept in touch all these years. He thought that my mindset was passive, since we were making a conscious decision to continue our connection.

The following spring break, I booked a flight to visit him in San Francisco without telling my parents. He took me to all his favorite spots, and we finally had a decent cup of coffee at Blue Bottle's garage. When we kissed goodbye at the airport, I had no idea that would be the last time I would ever see him.

Turns out James was right. Everything didn't happen for a reason. We were the ones making our connection last. Soon there were no more texts, packages, or plans. He's now married with a family. I guess we didn't fit into each other's lives, or maybe like music, we just were never on the same track.

What to Pack to See a Boy to Look Chill When You Have Zero Chill

---

- ☐ A low-key hoodie (or steal his)
- ☐ Badass jacket
- ☐ Your face (makeup bag)
- ☐ "I always sleep in these!" lingerie
- ☐ "Go sports!" sneakers
- ☐ "Are you my boyfriend?" jeans
- ☐ "Is he taller than me?" boots
- ☐ "I ate like a boy for the weekend" leggings
- ☐ "I swear I listen to this band" vintage T-shirt
- ☐ Basics you can mix and match
- ☐ #NoMakeup sunglasses
- ☐ TSA-approved toiletries
- ☐ "I'd love to meet your parents!" chambray
- ☐ Bobby pins and hair ties (to mark your territory)

BOY BINGO

Lives outside your zip code	**Talk on the phone more than you do in person**	**Most dates include at least an hour of travel**
Always busy	**Free space!**	**He's the last person you text at night and the first you text in the morning. (Besides your mom. That's normal, right?)**
Sends you letters, poems, and/or songs	**Send each other a lot of selfies**	**You and your phone have never been closer**

Quiz

WILL YOUR LONG-DISTANCE RELATIONSHIP LAST?

Do you have a solid foundation?

How's your communication?

Ⓐ Like a rock!

Ⓑ Kind of?

Ⓐ We talk almost every day!

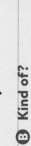

Ⓑ Not that consistent...

How's your chemistry in person?

Ⓐ On fire!

Ⓑ It's better over text.

Do you talk about the future?

Ⓐ All the time!

Ⓑ Not really...

Will you see each other IRL soon?

Ⓐ Flight is booked!

Ⓑ Not sure...

Mostly Ⓐ

This sounds promising! Keep up your excellent communication and keep making sure you're on the same page.

Mostly Ⓑ

This doesn't sound too promising, but it doesn't mean it can't work out. Try to communicate what you're feeling, and find out where he's at. What does he want? Where does he see this relationship going? Are you always the one reaching out and traveling to him, or is it mutual? With any type of relationship, being on the same page (or track) is key. In long-distance dating, seeing eye to eye can really make or break the relationship.

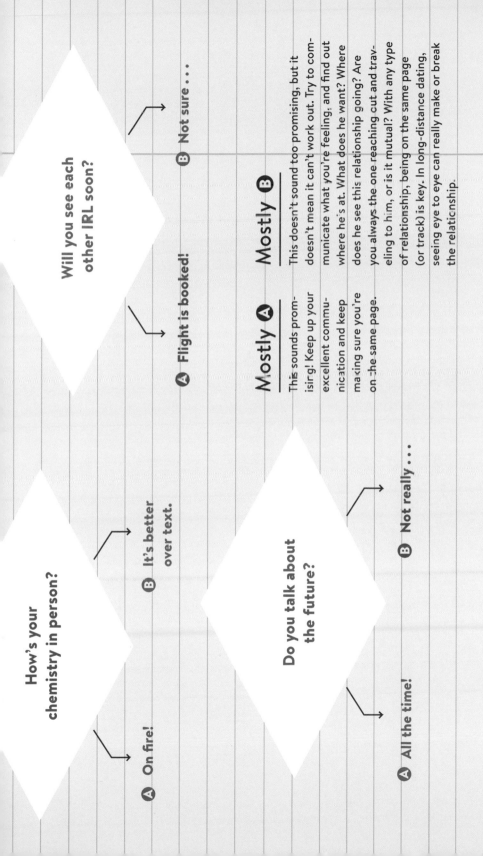

MIX TAPE

HOW TO MAKE THE PERFECT PLAYLIST

A BANGER
"We found Love" by Rihanna
featuring Calvin Harris

HIS SONG
"In My Feelings" by Drake

YOUR SONG
"Kiss Me" by
Sixpence None the Richer

#TBT
"I feel Love" by
Donna Summer

SOMETHING SWEET
"Dream A Little Dream of Me"
by The Mamas & The Papas

FILTHY RAP
"What's Your Fantasy" by
Ludacris (Featuring Shanna)

CHILL
"A Real Hero" by College,
with Electric Youth

SWITCH GENRE
"365" by Zedd & Katy Perry

DANCE
"Be My Lover"
by La Bouche

NEW FIND
"R U with Me"
by ASTR

**LEAVE HIM
WANTING MORE**
"Just Can't Get Enough"
by Depeche Mode

by DJ DENISE LOVE HEWETT @ deniselovehewett

Ask Someone Else

Guy I Dated: James, 34, casually dated long distance for about 3 years

I'm generally uncomfortable with published details about myself. I think I am largely okay with everything you have written, and candidly, I want to empower you to publish the most creative, honest thing you can. I don't want personal identifiable information about me out in the wild, but I am fine with you writing as you remember.

Couple: Jamie, 33, & Ryan, 34, together 9 years

You don't have to talk every hour of every day. Close-distance couples usually don't, so why should your relationship be any different? Don't pressure yourself or your partner with that exhausting expectation! The biggest challenge to making a long-distance relationship work is to avoid constantly comparing what might be better for you: the job, friends, and lifestyle you have now—or the job, friends, and lifestyle you'd have if you moved with them. You have to let go of the "what ifs" and realize "what is," and be satisfied, happy, and at peace with that. At some point, you're headed to them or they're headed to you (for us it was four years later), and that transition requires compromise, sacrifice, and selflessness.

Expert: Fabiola Wong, mindful communication coach, @FabiolaDWong

The only way to make things work in a long distance relationship is with effective communication. When you can't see or touch each other, you're forced to rely on digital forms of communication like text, phone calls, and FaceTime. If a long-distance couple gets into a fight, make-up sex isn't really a thing. Focus on having open conversations about expectations, thoughts, and emotions, with the purpose of working through the problems. The only way you'll know how to make each other happy is by talking about it!

4

THE
GUY YOU
ALWAYS GO
BACK TO

IT'LL BE DIFFERENT THIS TIME!

HEY, AT LEAST
YOU'RE RECYCLING

WE ARE NEVER, EVER
GETTING BACK
TOGETHER . . . JK!

t he first time I looked into Seth's kind hazel eyes, I knew he was the one. My parents, who have been together for decades, described a similar connection when they first met. After only a few months of dating over Chianti and spaghetti at a hole-in-the-wall Italian restaurant, Seth squeezed my arm and told me he was falling for me. My heart melted. I was falling for him, too.

The next afternoon on my lunch break from my retail job, I saw Seth across the street. I assumed he was bringing me an espresso, like he did last Saturday. When I'd asked him what for, he said, "Just because." No guy had ever been this self-less. He was probably on his way to see me again! I looked closer and noticed he was holding hands with a girl . . . I knew as his ex. I was sure there was a reason. But he walked right past me in silence. I went back to work and cried in the shoe closet until my manager yelled at me to come out. How could I sell skinny jeans under these circumstances?!

I frantically texted Seth asking what happened. He assured me he'd tell me in person. Later, as his eyes welled up, I assumed he was going to confess he got back with his ex. Instead he revealed, "I have a brain tumor."

Suddenly it all made sense. *Of course* he had a brain tumor. That's why he was with his ex-girlfriend. She was older, and they had dated for two years. She probably knew how to deal with this better than I could. I kissed his head, heartbroken that the love of my life was dying. Seth made me promise not to tell anyone. He was a senior, and moving to Los Angeles next semester for an internship. He was get-ting surgery over winter break to remove the tumor. He didn't want people to feel sorry for him.

When Seth left for California, we had a tearful goodbye. We agreed to stay in touch but not be together. It was just too much. I cried every day thinking about him balancing school, an internship, a new city across the country, and a brain tumor.

I was talking to my sorority sister who was in Los Angeles with Seth. I couldn't help but tell her about his brain tumor. She laughed. "Gabi, that's the biggest lie I've ever heard. If Seth was recover-ing from a brain tumor he wouldn't be

TASTE:	LOOK:	SOUND:	SMELL:	FEEL:
That big tub of frozen yogurt with all of the toppings and flavors, which always hurts your stomach after	The same as he did when you fell for him years ago	"Edge of Desire" by John Mayer	The musk of an old, worn, deeply loved book	Anxious he's going to break your heart all over again

partying this hard." I was heartbroken. I started a Facebook group called "I Hate Liars," and sang "I Will Survive" at karaoke every chance I got. But deep down I was crushed and doubted I'd ever love again.

I wish I could tell you that was the last time I ever spoke to Seth. But two years later I moved to Los Angeles, and we reconnected. He apologized profusely for everything he'd put me through. He assured me his feelings for me were always real, but he hadn't been ready for a relationship. So he told this inexcusable lie to justify why he was still with his ex. Eventually, after seeing Seth was working on becoming a better person, I accepted his apology, and our love grew deeper than a tasteless lie. Today, he is one of my best friends.

Seth and I have been off and on for ten years now. I'd get boyfriends, he'd get girlfriends. I still compare him to every guy I date. Often the guys I date don't accept me for who I am. Seth was (is!) the only person who always saw me for me and not some idea of me. Over the years, there were glimmers of hope for us, but he never chose me. When I packed up my life in Los Angeles to move in with my boyfriend in Brooklyn, Seth was crushed. "Are you going to marry this guy?" he asked. I thought so.

But my New York love story ended. I moved back home to Los Angeles. I don't know what the future holds for Seth and me. While it may sound masochistic, sometimes deep down I wonder if he's the person for me. For better or worse, right? Even when friends constantly remind me, "*Gabi. He lied to you about having a brain tumor.*" Which was wrong, but after all these years I am able to forgive Seth's lie. As long as he was never lying about loving me.

Reduce vs. Reuse vs. Recycle

Reduce

Limit your contact with him.

Cut back on the times you go over to his place when you know you shouldn't.

Stop crying over the fact that it's always the same.

Lower the number of times you look at old pictures of him and mourn what was.

Reuse

Repurpose the shirt he left at your place. Now it's a cute gym tank with ample side boob!

Give that nice guy another shot, and don't compare him to you know who.

Rewrite your love story; pay attention to what hurts instead of just the highlight reel.

Make new memories at your favorite bar, restaurant, or any other place you associate with him.

Recycle

The bottle of wine you drank last night as you cried over him.

Remember, this relationship is hazardous to your heart, and therefore hard to recycle.

Avoid getting into toxic relationships whenever possible.

BOY BINGO

You always, *always*, get back together	You tell people he's your Mr. Big	You believe you'll end up together
You constantly check in on him on social media	Free space! 	You have drunk dialed or tipsy texted him many times
You compare everyone you date to him	He made you ugly cry at least once	You loved him, and probably still love him

Quiz

WILL IT BE DIFFERENT THIS TIME?

Have you had an honest and thoughtful conversation about what went wrong, and how it will be different this time?

Ⓐ Over drinks! I'm sure he'll remember!

Ⓑ We did. We're both in therapy and/or are working on ourselves.

Are you able to let go of the past and live in the present?

Ⓐ Totally. But seriously, can you believe what he did last time? Deep down, I'm worried he'll do that again.

Ⓑ We're speaking only in present tense, and it feels nice!

Are you both on the same page in terms of what you want and where you see this relationship going?

Ⓐ I see us getting engaged in a year. He isn't ready for marriage any time soon, but I'm pretty sure if I'm patient, he'll change his mind.

Ⓑ We both are ready to be in this relationship and see it going the same way.

Do you trust him?

Ⓐ Not really!

Ⓑ Yes. I am finally over what happened in the past and ready for our new chapter.

What do your friends and family think about you rekindling your love?

Ⓐ They're tired of hearing the same stories. But it'll be different this time!

Ⓑ They're happy I'm happy and agree this time it feels different. But if he hurts me again, they will probably "curse the day he was born."

Mostly Ⓐ

It sounds like you still have baggage from the past that will make it difficult for you and your partner to continue. Communication is key. Make sure you are both on the same page. Talk about what you both expect from this relationship before you try it again.

Mostly Ⓑ

Looks like you both have really grown and are sharing your feelings and expectations! Change has been made, the past is in the past, and it could work out this time around. Keep up the honesty and communication, and things really could be different this time!

Ask Someone Else

Guy I Dated: Seth, 33, dated on and off for 8 years

———

I'm sad that most of our story is about the brain tumor when it was so much deeper than that. When you care about someone—and you keep going back to them—I think you need to have a real conversation defining what's going on and getting on the same page about your feelings. If the person is someone who's worthwhile as a lover or a friend, they will hear you and be open to a relationship. If they can't hear you, then the relationship isn't worth going back to. All of the problems occur due to miscommunication and dishonesty.

Couple: Shawn, 26, & Jared, 26, together 3 years

———

Really ask yourself if the stress of being on-and-off is worth it. If you're not 100 percent sure about the person, sometimes it's best to just walk away. It doesn't make you or the other person "bad," it just means walking away

from something bringing you anxiety. You deserve to have someone who makes you feel determined to make it work. Every couple has their bumps, but ultimately it is the knowledge that this person is worth pushing through all the bullshit that keeps you going. If you're not sure if they're worth the effort, just know it is your gut telling you something won't click.

Expert: Rachel Russo, MS, MFT, matchmaker, dating and relationship coach, author of *How to Get Over Your Ex: A Step by Step Guide to Mend a Broken Heart— Italian American Style*

———

As someone who has gotten back with exes multiple times—there might even be one ex I would get back with now—you have to figure out what went wrong in your relationship and what has changed. What is going to be different this time around? So to

many, this requires going to therapy—maybe for one or both people—and really coming up with a strategic plan. If no one is committed to change, then it won't work. You have to treat your relationship like it's new. I have seen way too many people spending too much time on one person and having false hope.

5

THE GUY WITH AN EXPIRATION DATE

MET ON VACATION

YOU'RE MOVING

MR. RIGHT NOW

When I was a junior in college, my boyfriend Ryan and I had a song. It was "Slow Dancing in a Burning Room" by John Mayer. He didn't know it was about a failing relationship. I did but was thrilled to finally have a boyfriend who let our song be by my all-time favorite musician.

Growing up in Connecticut in the early 2000s, I thought I was doomed to end up with a certain type of guy. He'd have spiked hair and wear electric blue button-downs and puka shell necklaces. He'd smell like a shopping mall. You know that cross between Abercrombie & Fitch's Fierce cologne and freshly baked Cinnabons? When I met Ryan, I was relieved he wasn't this type. He was tall, with Midwestern manners and hair that swept across his face like Jim Halpert's.

On our first date, over oysters, I started to fall for Ryan: how his laugh boomed at all my jokes, his eyes sparkled under his shaggy hair, and his perfect smile brightened up the dim candlelit restaurant. I don't know if it was the aphrodisiac from the fresh seafood, or how he had the familiar scent of marine breeze and sandalwood, but when he kissed me, we felt like one, despite having little in common.

Ryan had just moved to Boston for a job in finance. No matter the season he wore pastel button-downs. He followed sports, enjoyed beer, and loved everything about Beantown—from its dive bars to its cobblestone streets.

I, on the other hand, couldn't wait to get out of Boston and get a job in Los Angeles. No matter the season, I wore heels. I hated sports, thought beer was gross, and despised everything about Beantown. Especially how people called it "Beantown."

One night we stumbled into a convenience store and became entranced by a dusty jar of pickled lemons. We couldn't stop laughing at this bizarre condiment. Through my tears of laughter and his booming chuckle, I found myself falling deeply in love with Ryan.

But despite my love for Ryan, I was consumed with college and getting out of Boston as soon as possible. I knew I'd have to choose between Ryan and my career, and my career would inevitably win.

One day Ryan told me he had to go into Abercrombie & Fitch to get more cologne. I thought he was joking, but he wasn't. Soon I realized that the familiar marine breeze and sandalwood scent from

TASTE:	LOOK:	SOUND:	SMELL:	FEEL:
Expired milk	Somebody that you used to know	The beep of a timer	Like you have to throw something out of your fridge, but you don't know what	You miss him, but he's right in front of you

our first date actually was Abercrombie & Fitch's signature Fierce cologne. Perhaps those pheromones really do work.

Senior year, Ryan was supposed to help me and my parents move me out of my apartment and into another one. But the day before the move, he decided to go to the Hamptons with friends. My parents were pissed. I realized it was better to end things now and spend my last year of college fully focused on myself. It didn't make sense to stay in a relationship where it felt like I was growing, and he wasn't growing with me. Especially since this relationship would have to end in a couple of months anyway when I moved to Los Angeles.

So I ended things, saying I needed to focus on making the most of my senior year. Ryan was heartbroken but understood. A couple of months later he emailed me confessing, "There hasn't been a day that goes by that I don't think about you." I was thinking about him, too.

When I moved to Los Angeles, he texted me, "If money wasn't an issue, would you consider moving in with me in Iowa, and someday getting married?" I wanted to fly to Iowa and greet him with a hug and a jar of pickled lemons, but deep down I knew Ryan didn't fit into my life anymore. So, I told him the truth: I moved to Los Angeles for my career, not to find a husband.

That was ten years ago. Now he's living in Iowa, married with a family of his own. Honestly, I'm happy for Ryan. I think about him after breakups, wondering, what if I had married him? But then I think about how happy and full my life is now, and I don't regret it. As hard as it is, sometimes you have to accept expiration when it comes to dating. Just like we never tried that expired jar of pickled lemons, there are times you can't be tempted to give a relationship that's over another taste.

How to Make It Work Past the Expiration Date

———

Encourage each other to pursue your health goals, both physical and mental. It can be small, like eating plant-based foods for a week, or big, like training for a marathon together.

Be adventurous, maybe in the bedroom, or just in life together. Go out of your comfort zone, break your patterns, try something new.

Give each other space and "me time" when you can. Sometimes a little distance every now and then can help your relationship grow and thrive.

Celebrate the small stuff in a big way. Toast to achievements as a couple as well as individual accomplishments.

Admit when you're wrong, and don't be afraid to say you're sorry. Don't keep score. Remember, you're on each other's team.

Remember to turn on the romance once in a while, especially when things get too comfortable. Little thoughtful "just because" gestures go a long way.

Make each other's friends feel welcome. You don't have to love them, but you should respect them.

Cheer each other on! Encourage your partner to reach his goals. Always offer support and solutions (not criticism) along the way.

BOY BINGO

Met on vacation	He's moving	You're moving
You've outgrown each other	Free space!	Soon you'll be long distance

Said goodbye more times than you can count, but you're still holding on	Want different things in life	Know there's no future

WILL THIS WORK OUT IN THE LONG TERM?

Since you started dating, have you or your partner made any changes for the better?

Ⓐ Yeah! We really are growing together.

Ⓑ Not so much. Sometimes I feel like I'm growing and my partner is staying the same.

When you think about losing him, how do you feel?

Ⓐ Devastated. I can't imagine life without him. It would feel like I lost a part of myself.

Ⓑ I would be sad, but ultimately I would survive.

When you fight, what's more important?

Ⓐ Coming up with a compromise or solution to whatever we're arguing about.

Ⓑ Being right.

Does it feel like someone supports the other more?

Ⓐ We support each other equally.

Ⓑ Yeah . . .

How are you when you're apart?

Ⓐ Great! We have amazing communication.

Ⓑ We get into fights. We're great when we're together though!

Mostly Ⓐ

It sounds like you have a solid foundation to make this work! Your expiration date might just be an obstacle on the long road of your relationship.

Mostly Ⓑ

If you want this to work, both of you will have to start making changes. Remember, relationships are work, and you both have to put the work in. So unless you are both okay having an expiration date, start having those honest conversations.

Ask Someone Else

Guy I Dated: Ryan, 35, dated for 9 months

Reading this has been a little tough. I don't want to email or talk about this anymore. I hope your book is a success.

Couple: Monica, 30, & Miguel, 36, together 8 years

I had just graduated college and was about to move to Spain to teach English. The last thing my mom said to me when she dropped me off at the airport was, "Don't fall in love. Remember that you have to come back home."

I met Miguel, my now-husband of eight years, the first night I was in town. I didn't think too much about him, except that I liked his confidence. We were friends for a while, and then we hooked up. A year after meeting, he told me he didn't want to be without me. He told me he loved me and would marry me, if I would have him. We got married sixteen months after meeting.

Our expiration date created a sense of urgency. It brought us to a crossroads. My life changed the moment I said yes. It's been eight years and two kids later.

Go with your gut. Think about this person not being in your life. How would you handle that? Does it feel like you would be missing a literal part of yourself or would you just miss the person? Sometimes we're with people because we don't have enough confidence in ourselves to step outside our comfort zones. So, be proactive about love and about what's best for you. If it doesn't feel right then why are you even with that person? Use an expiration date more like a deadline to make a decision as to whether or not you want to continue sharing your life with that one person.

Expert: Mrs. Honeycutt, my high school guidance counselor

I do not believe that anyone can "make a relationship work." It's either there or it's not. In my opinion, a woman should never compromise herself for a guy. Think about Ruth Bader Ginsburg. Her husband relocated to Washington to further her opportunities. There needs to be that mutual respect. Most of the time, high school relationships end naturally when two people go off to different colleges or have different plans. Be true to yourself. It is important for twenty-somethings to evolve into the people they are going to become. The human brain does not fully develop until around the age of 25 or 26, so many decisions that are made before this age are not the best ones.

6

THE GUY WHO'S YOUR INSTANT BOYFRIEND

SUDDENLY, YOU'RE AT IKEA

EASY TO ASSEMBLE AND BREAK APART!

QUICK! WHAT ARE HIS
PARENTS' NAMES?

henry and I were on the hunt for a peach A-line dress and a men's leather jacket. We were going as zombie Jennifer Grey and Patrick Swayze á la *Dirty Dancing*. It was too soon. Not only for a couple's costume (we'd been dating for only a month), but because it was Halloween 2009. Patrick Swayze had died not even a month before, and Jennifer Grey's career, like our joke implied, was indeed dead (this was before her triumphant 2010 *Dancing with the Stars* comeback).

"Too soon" was the theme of our relationship. But I felt instantly comfortable with Henry. He had the face of a kid in a Norman Rockwell painting: earnest, reliable, and full of wonder. We both were pursuing comedy, so a lot of our relationship felt like a bit. We just kept yes, and . . .-ing each other until we became boyfriend and girlfriend. "Yes, and . . . " is a rule-of-thumb in improvisational comedy. It means you should always accept what your scene partner says (yes) and then expand on it (and . . .). "Yes, and . . . " can be supportive in dating, as long as you stay grounded. Henry and I were not grounded, as evidenced by the time I asked if we were exclusive,

and he said, "Yes, and . . . We should probably make it Facebook official!" And that's how Henry and I went from strangers to "in a Facebook relationship" in under a month. Now you never have to take an improv class! You're welcome.

When I moved into my first Los Angeles apartment, Henry agreed not only to come to Ikea with me but also to help assemble my furniture. As we were putting together my white Leirvik bed frame, I started to realize I didn't know Henry's favorite food. Or what he wanted to be when he grew up. Or his parents' names. We had been dating in the fast lane for two months, and I didn't really know Henry.

The more I got to know Henry, the more I realized we weren't compatible. So much of our relationship was just us. Alone we made sense, but out in the world, we didn't. While we were both pursuing comedy, our senses of humor didn't gel. Then I started to realize the other things that didn't match, like our friends, taste in music, or favorite foods. The only thing we seemed to have in common was that we both wanted a significant other.

TASTE:	LOOK:	SOUND:	SMELL:	FEEL:
Microwavable dinner that hasn't been fully defrosted, but you're starving so you eat it anyway	Warm, safe, and comfortable	The whiz of race cars	The pieces of new furniture before you assemble them	Like a boyfriend pillow, but he's a real boy!

After some time apart on a work trip, I realized I had to break up with Henry. So I wore my best break-up outfit, which is a lot of accessories to really validate the whole "It's not you, it's me" argument. Of course, it's me, I'm wearing two belts! He took it surprisingly well. As he tearfully hugged me goodbye, he asked the weighted question: "What should we do about our Facebook relationship?" I told him since we weren't dating anymore, we should probably get rid of it. He told me I could end it. Whenever I was ready.

Later, when I got home, I logged on to Facebook only to find I was in a relationship . . . with no one? He broke his promise, unfriended me, and blocked me. Which I guess was fitting. I never really knew Henry to begin with, so in a way, I was always in a Facebook relationship with no one.

When I was writing this, I contacted Henry on LinkedIn (he had blocked me everywhere else). He's far more successful than I am now, and I'm happy for him. Not only in work, but he told me he's been married for five years (while I can barely hold on to a relationship for five months). I'm grateful I dated Henry. Being with him reminded me how important it is to really know the guy you're dating before making it official. Your instant boyfriend and Ikea furniture can last, but only if you assemble both properly.

Signs You Should Slow Down

One—or both—of you still has a lot of work to do on yourself. Perhaps you just got out of a relationship. You haven't taken the time to step back and do the necessary work needed to properly move on.

You are inseparable. All of your other relationships are being sacrificed because you are spending all your time and energy with this person. Even when you're not together, you're not present. You're glued to your phone talking to your new love.

After a short time, your lives are already intertwined. You're always at each other's places and have even considered moving in together. You've been dating for only a couple of months.

Your friends and family are skeptical. They might see red flags you don't. Or they also notice this is happening too fast.

You say "I love you," but you're not sure you love him yet. Are you just saying it to be polite? Do you really know him? You might need more time to really get to know this person before hitting the "I love you" crosswalk.

BOY BINGO

Less than a month and you're already boyfriend and girlfriend	You're inseparable	Your PDA makes others uncomfortable
Met each other's friends and family	Free space!	Already refer to each other by pet names like "Babe," "Shnookums," and/or "Poopy"
Have brunch without alcohol, which, for the record, is breakfast	You post photos of each other	Keep more than a toothbrush at each other's places 

Quiz

IS IT TOO SOON?

How much "me time" do you get in this relationship?

Ⓐ None! We spend all our time together and I love it! Who needs "me time" when you have "we time"?!

Ⓑ Enough. We think it's important for us to each have our own experiences and growth outside the relationship.

Be honest, why are you in this relationship?

Ⓐ Because I really wanted a boyfriend, and there he was! Love happens when you least expect it, right?

Ⓑ I wasn't looking to get into a relationship, but my boyfriend has been so supportive and wonderful. Love happens when you least expect it, right?

Your best friend has one extra ticket to a sold-out show of your favorite band. What do you do?

Ⓐ Aw, I'd have to pass. I can't leave the BF alone on date night!

Ⓑ Go! When else is this opportunity going to come up? The old ball and chain will understand.

How long have you been dating?

Ⓐ Less than three months, but I just really feel like he's the one!

Ⓑ More than three months.

How often do you talk about the future?

Ⓐ Not a ton, but we love each other, so we'll totally make it work. All you need is love, right?

Ⓑ A lot. We both know what the other wants out of life, and our hopes and dreams align.

Mostly Ⓐ

It's too soon! This doesn't mean your relationship can't work; just try to take a step back. If you can build a strong foundation, this can work out. Challenge yourself to spend time apart. It will only make things more special when you're together.

Mostly Ⓑ

Seems like you've been giving this relationship a strong foundation and also space to breathe. Everything about this seems healthy so far. Keep it up, and remember that relationships are work.

Ask Someone Else

Guy I Dated: Henry, 32, dated 2 months

Gabi broke up with me after I picked her up from the airport. That was the last time we spoke . . . until she emailed me for this quote.

Couple: Jessie, 34, & Nathaniel, 34, together 5 years

Nathaniel and I went from just meeting to just married in five months, so I guess he was my instant-husband! Here we are five years later and with a baby, and we couldn't be happier. It's super easy to get carried away by the romance of an overnight relationship and not consider the practical aspects, or even worse, decide to disregard any red flags in favor of keeping the fairy tale alive. Though we certainly raced to the altar, we had already discussed religion, children (how many and how to raise them), career hopes, values, family dynamics, finances, how we would handle terminal illness/layoffs/unexpected tragedy, our desires for travel, and where we would ultimately like to buy or build a house. We would take long walks and hikes and just talk for hours. I managed to feel closer to him in those few short months than I had with others in years, and by the time we tied the knot, I knew not only intuitively ("when you know, you know") but practically that he was completely on the same page with what I wanted for our future. Trust your gut but talk it out to exhaustion, and when someone shows you who they are, believe them.

Expert: Will Siu, MD, psychiatrist

Most people choose attachment over authenticity. We live in a Western world that has seen increasingly disingenuous relationships and shunned traditional community, and we have seen parents spend less time with their children due to professional ambitions. These and other societal patterns have resulted in emotionally immature adults who struggle to relate authentically to others. In object relations theory, the drive of the psyche seeking reparations for relationships can lead to unhealthy or seemingly irrational romantic relationship patterns over genuine connections to try to overcome the unconscious psychic pain of early immature object relations. Early powerful and unexplainable attraction to partners we barely know can often be a sign of prioritizing attachment reparations over authentic connections.

7

THE GUY WHO TEXTS "SUP" AT 2 a.m.

SENDS DICK PICS

SLIDES INTO YOUR DMs

POOR? (CAN'T TAKE
YOU OUT ON
A REAL DATE)

i finally convinced Josh to take me to brunch. We had been dating for a couple of weeks, but I never saw him in daylight. I started to wonder if he was a vampire. Is that why he loved *Buffy the Vampire Slayer*?

The plan was we'd get brunch, and then he'd drive me home. I was a little surprised when he pulled into a shopping center. But then I remembered that some of the best sushi restaurants in Los Angeles were in shopping centers. Maybe the same was true with brunch spots?

Then we walked into a Chipotle. My heart sank. This was not the hour-long sit-down with eggs Benedict and mimosas flowing that I had imagined. But I figured burritos and Coronas could count as brunch! Until I noticed Josh ordered his burrito bowl to go. I didn't get anything. It was too late. My brunch dreams were shattered, like the shell from the eggs of the frittata I'd never share with Josh.

It hadn't always been like this. Josh used to be my friend who'd crack me up with jokes, ask me about my day, and was always supportive. Deep down, I had a crush on Josh. I liked how our conversations felt like a never-ending ping-pong game. I found his style of jeans, Converse, and graphic T-shirts low-key dreamy.

When Henry (Instant Boyfriend) and I broke up, Josh treated me to Stellas at a neon-lit bar. We kissed. The whole thing felt like that part in *When Harry Met Sally* when you see why men and women (who are both attracted to each other) can't be friends.

I was confused about what was happening. Here was a guy who had become my friend, and now I was attracted to him, and he was attracted to me. So we should probably date, right?

Wrong. Josh couldn't be clearer that he did not want a girlfriend. But any time we were both available, we couldn't help but be together. Our chemistry was that good!

Soon Josh stopped being the friend who asked me how my day was going at 2 p.m. and started being the guy who texted me "sup" at 2 a.m.

There was a power Josh held over me when he texted me those three letters: all lowercase, no question mark, at last call. I'd always go over. If I wasn't drinking, I'd drive on an empty tank of gas, and have to do the gas pump of shame in the morning. With each encounter, I'd hope that I'd prove something to Josh. Prove that I was worthy of his undivided attention.

TASTE:	LOOK:	SOUND:	SMELL:	FEEL:
Late-night pizza	A default picture with a girl obviously cropped out	A bartender belting, "Last call!"	Sweat and the whisper of body odor from a night out	Wanted but unfulfilled

Soon I realized that to Josh I would always be a booty call and never a girl-friend. I was upset at first. But I eventually accepted it for what it was. In my head, Josh was forever single, always comfortable, and consistent. He was living in the same two-bedroom apartment, watching the same reruns of *Buffy the Vampire Slayer*, with not even a bobby pin of evidence of another girl in his life.

When I sent Josh this story, I was shocked he called me immediately after reading it. And it was 5:30 p.m. when we chatted! In the close to eight years that Josh and I hooked up off and on, I don't think we ever spoke on the phone. "You hate it," I sighed. He laughed. "No! I don't hate it. I'm sorry. I'm so sorry I put you through that all those years. I was really a jerk." My heart skipped a beat. Finally, the validation I needed, eight years too late.

Looking back, The Guy Who Texts You "sup" at 2 a.m. can be fun, especially when you're on the same page. If you want more, know that you deserve better than "sup." Know you are worthy of a boyfriend, a brunch, and a guy who wants to hang out in broad daylight. You might not see it now, but there's a guy out there who will text you at 2 a.m. just to ask you how your day was.

Fun and Flirty Texts to Send After the Last Call That Might Get a Text Back

Some of these are cruel, so please use with caution.

Want to make out?

Hey, um . . . when was the last time you got tested?

FaceTime request. He might not pick up, but he'll likely text to make sure you're okay. Same works with a phone call.

I have wine!

I found a 🐱 / 🐶. Come over!

So . . . I didn't get my period.

BOY BINGO

You never hang out in daylight	You never text sober	You never make plans to hang out
He sent you at least one dick pic	Free space!	It's mostly sexual

Never been on a real date	Never met his friends, but know he has friends	It's not work, and that's kind of nice

Quiz

CAN YOU TURN YOUR BOOTY CALL INTO A BOYFRIEND?

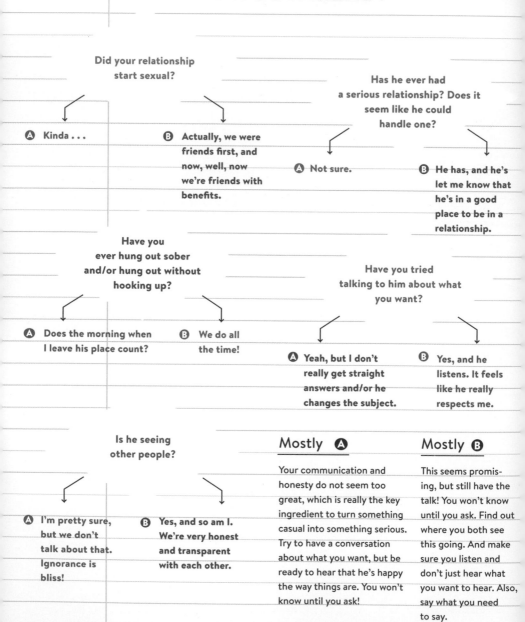

Did your relationship start sexual?

Ⓐ Kinda . . .

Ⓑ Actually, we were friends first, and now, well, now we're friends with benefits.

Has he ever had a serious relationship? Does it seem like he could handle one?

Ⓐ Not sure.

Ⓑ He has, and he's let me know that he's in a good place to be in a relationship.

Have you ever hung out sober and/or hung out without hooking up?

Ⓐ Does the morning when I leave his place count?

Ⓑ We do all the time!

Have you tried talking to him about what you want?

Ⓐ Yeah, but I don't really get straight answers and/or he changes the subject.

Ⓑ Yes, and he listens. It feels like he really respects me.

Is he seeing other people?

Ⓐ I'm pretty sure, but we don't talk about that. Ignorance is bliss!

Ⓑ Yes, and so am I. We're very honest and transparent with each other.

Mostly Ⓐ

Your communication and honesty do not seem too great, which is really the key ingredient to turn something casual into something serious. Try to have a conversation about what you want, but be ready to hear that he's happy the way things are. You won't know until you ask!

Mostly Ⓑ

This seems promising, but still have the talk! You won't know until you ask. Find out where you both see this going. And make sure you listen and don't just hear what you want to hear. Also, say what you need to say.

Ask Someone Else

Guy I Dated: Josh, 34, booty call for 8 years, on and off

I'm so sorry you went through that. I had no idea we were on such different pages. Apologies. Also, you know what's weird? I just started rewatching *Buffy the Vampire Slayer*. Holds up.

Couple: Kristen, 32, & Niko, 31, together 6 years (officially)

Don't be scared to be open about your feelings, and don't play games. Not worth it. My mom always said, "If you like someone, don't be scared to admit it. What's the worst that can happen? You find out they don't like you? That's better than not knowing and wasting your time. If you want to text him, just text him. Who cares who texted last?" We make our relationship work because we were so open from the beginning—whenever there is something bothering us or we are uncomfortable with a situation, we talk about it right away.

We were always open and honest. Maybe too honest. I think we both always knew the other was the one. Deep down, I pretty much felt secure in where I stood with Niko. It all just kind of happened organically and nothing felt forced. —Kristen

Be patient. Period. We aren't patient anymore with anything we do, and I think that's why a lot of people find it hard to build and maintain relationships. But the truth is, it really is about the journey and growing. Respecting each other's needs and wants is most important. —Niko

Expert: Anthony Recenello, dating and relationship mentor

I think women are taught that a guy either wants a relationship or just a hookup. And if you put yourself into the hookup category, then you lose the chance of him wanting anything more. If the two people have a ton of chemistry together, they can both grow an attachment to one other.

You should focus on how much fun you're having and how much you two connect. When a guy texts you "sup" at 2 a.m., it could mean anything. It could mean he's drunk at a bar and is looking to cuddle with someone when he gets home. But it also could mean he's been trying not to text you all day and finally got the courage to say something after a few drinks. Don't look too much into it. There is no guaranteed way to win a specific man's heart. Men, just like women, have preferences. Here's what you can do, and this is what I teach my clients in my Soulmate Method program: 1. Write down specific ideas of who you want to be with. 2. Find and then move toward only those types of men. 3. Filter out all men showing red flags. 4. Stay completely positive and confident all throughout.

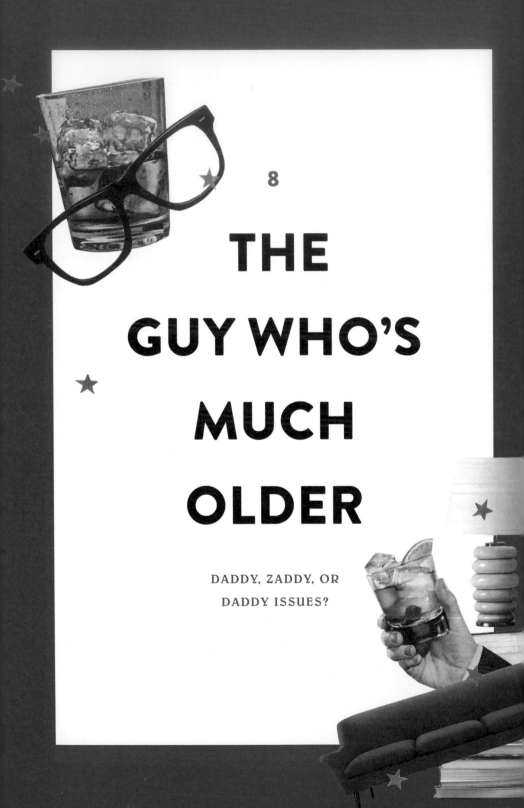

8

THE GUY WHO'S MUCH OLDER

DADDY, ZADDY, OR
DADDY ISSUES?

Our first date was at an Italian restaurant that projected Fellini films on the wall as techno music bumped (in other words, a very authentic Italian restaurant). Over bucatini and grenache wine, I found myself fascinated by Robert. There was something brooding and mysterious about him, like an actor in a CW show. He impressed me with his love and appreciation for films (which I hadn't yet realized was a common trait among men in Hollywood), and I impressed him with my love and appreciation for solid foods (which I kind of knew was an uncommon trait among women in Los Angeles).

After dinner, we went to his bungalow, where he serenaded me with "Blackbird" on his guitar. I sang along, and just as he was about to go in for a kiss, I asked him his age. He told me he was 35. This was older than any guy I had ever dated, but I didn't care. I was 23 and ready to date a man.

We dated for almost a year. I met his friends; he met my family. He taught me about the finer things in life, like wine, French cuisine, and classic cinema. His favorite movie was *Lolita*. He lent me his favorite vintage baby blue T-shirt. I slept in it most nights. We talked about moving in together, getting engaged, and living happily ever after.

One night when we were getting ready for bed, he was in the bathroom and asked me to pick out a movie on his iPad. I asked him what his passcode was, and he told me it was his birthday.

I froze. How did I not know my boyfriend of almost a year's birthday?! Then I saw his wallet sitting on the nightstand. I had no choice but to check his ID. I didn't want him to come out of the bathroom without a movie picked!

I found his license and his birthday: April 23. My eyes moved to the year: 1966. I'm dyslexic, so I had to use the calculator on my phone. He was 45.

I asked him if he was really 45. He assured me that they made a mistake at the DMV. I knew this was a lie. They don't make mistakes at the DMV—that's why the lines are so long!

"I thought you knew," he finally sighed, which is another lie since I wrote him a card with thirty-six reasons why I loved him for what I thought was his thirty-sixth birthday. He never said, "Hey, Babe, looks like you need nine more!"

TASTE:	LOOK:	SOUND:	SMELL:	FEEL:
Cigars	Hair on his head is a different color than the hair on his body . . .	The tick of the clock in 60 *Minutes*	Aftershave and a high SPF	So young

I went to sleep hoping I'd wake up to find out it was all a bad dream. But it wasn't.

Whenever I tell people this story, they always ask me the same question: *How did you not know?!* I guess there were signs; I just ignored them. Like how all his photos from his twenties were printed out or why his favorite movie was *Lolita*. It now made sense why waiters always said "God bless you," after carding him. I thought it was because he looked good for 35. Turns out he looked *really* good for 45.

I didn't break up with him right away. I gave it a month. I made a pros and cons list. Pro: He treats me well. Con: He might be a sociopath. I knew what I had to do.

We had drinks. He took a sip of his scotch on the rocks.

Scotch?! How did I not notice this?

Tears streamed down my face. I told him I couldn't do this anymore.

As we waited for our cars, he gave me a tight hug. I reached into my bag to grab cash for the valet when I felt something soft. It was his vintage T-shirt. I handed it back to him. He told me to keep it.

When I got home, I finally read the back of the shirt: It said, "Don't let reality spoil your dreams." That seemed to be Robert's life motto. Not letting the reality of his age spoil his dreams of the perfect Hollywood life.

Then I turned 31. And I understood. At first, I felt ashamed of being an age where social media tells me I should be married with kids by now. Then I realized age really is just a number. Don't let the reality of something like your age spoil your dreams. Also, always card your boyfriend.

MEN IN THEIR 20s vs. MEN IN THEIR 30s vs. MEN IN THEIR 40s

20s	30s	40s
1. Loves doing shots!	1. Can navigate his way through a wine list with confidence	1. Loves scotch
2. Has roommates	2. Lives alone	2. Owns a home!
3. Sleepovers every night, spooning all night in his twin-size bed	3. Spoons you for an appropriate amount of time and then rolls over to his side of the queen bed	3. Rarely spoons you in his California king–size bed with memory foam; you're too comfortable to notice
4. Dinner date usually involves fast food	4. Dinner date means at a nice restaurant	4. Always orders takeout, because he hates going out

ALL: Doesn't know what to do when he has a cold

BOY BINGO

Takes a lot of medication and/or vitamins	**Has a wine collection**	**Wows waiters when they card him after you**
Enjoys museums, theater, jazz clubs, and/or the opera	**Free space!** 	**No digital photos of his 20s**
Most forms of technology confuse him	**Friends with names like Gertrude, Abe, and Beatrice— no, they're not hipsters**	**Can't start his day without NPR**

Quiz

IS HE TOO OLD FOR YOU?

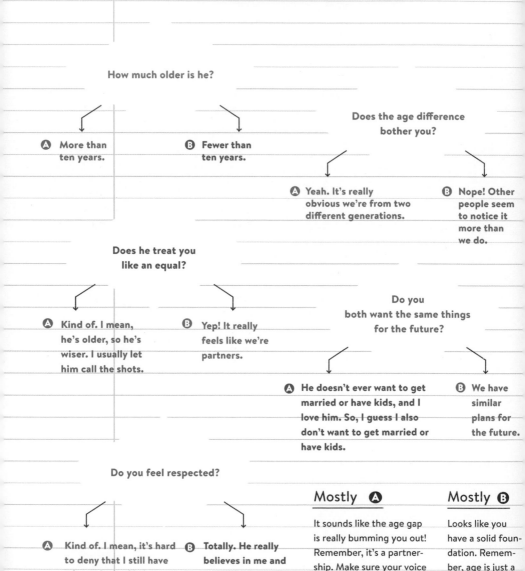

How much older is he?

(A) More than ten years.

(B) Fewer than ten years.

Does the age difference bother you?

(A) Yeah. It's really obvious we're from two different generations.

(B) Nope! Other people seem to notice it more than we do.

Does he treat you like an equal?

(A) Kind of. I mean, he's older, so he's wiser. I usually let him call the shots.

(B) Yep! It really feels like we're partners.

Do you both want the same things for the future?

(A) He doesn't ever want to get married or have kids, and I love him. So, I guess I also don't want to get married or have kids.

(B) We have similar plans for the future.

Do you feel respected?

(A) Kind of. I mean, it's hard to deny that I still have a lot to learn. He just knows better because he's older.

(B) Totally. He really believes in me and supports me.

Mostly (A)

It sounds like the age gap is really bumming you out! Remember, it's a partnership. Make sure your voice is heard, and you're treated like an equal. If he continues to infantilize you, cut your losses and run!

Mostly (B)

Looks like you have a solid foundation. Remember, age is just a number as long as you're treated like an equal.

Ask Someone Else

Guy I Dated: Robert, 53, dated for 9 months

I would prefer you not write a chapter about me, but as long as my name and obvious details are left out pertaining to my identity, I suppose you can do whatever you want creatively.

Couple: Andrea, 29, & Dan, 35, together 12 years

I met Dan when I was 17; he was 23, and I felt weird about it at first. I remember telling my mom that I knew I wanted to marry a man like Dan one day. Everyone's major concern when we got married (I was 21 and he was 27) was that we'd grow apart as we grew up. But it just boils down to this: No one else would care for me as much as he does; I know that through and through, without a doubt. The other stuff just kind of works out. Find someone who makes you feel like you have value on this planet, and you deserve to take up space. Don't have a list of must-haves. I think too many women (and men) want butterflies and fairy tales, and they just don't exist, not after a year or so, at least. You will always grow to hate the way he chews or how he snores. He'll get fat and ugly (so will you). But feeling valued and respected and loved will never get old. That's what gets you through. I married using common sense, and it was the best decision I've ever made. —Andrea

Early on, our age difference was often a challenge, but that went away with time. We are sort of opposites that attract, which also comes with its own challenges. While it's important to be attracted to each other, that shouldn't be the primary or main theme of the relationship. —Dan

Experts: Lauren Rosenberg & Jaydi Samuels, LJMatchmaking

Our advice for a twenty-something girl dating an older man is to be sure he isn't too set in his ways. Being single for too long might cause a person to fall into a routine: a routine they are unwilling to part with once you enter their life. Get a sense of what his relationship experience has been, and why previous partnerships haven't worked out for him. What has he learned from his exes? Do you find he speaks about his exes in a respectful way? Does he have commitment issues, or has he simply not found the right person yet? Don't be intimidated by his age, and remind yourself what value and life experiences you bring to the relationship. Be sure you have enough in common. Is he mature and stable, and is his age adding value to your relationship, or taking away from it?

9

THE GUY WHO'S COOLER THAN YOU

THE ARTIST
YOU SUPPORT

WOKE BRO

PROBABLY HAS A
SHOE COLLECTION

i cut my Christmas trip home short to meet my boyfriend Andres back in Los Angeles. The plan was to spend a night in West Hollywood, and then head to Hawaii to ring in the New Year. He assured me we could fly there standby no problem because his roommate's uncle was a pilot.

When I arrived at LAX, I noticed my "just landed" text to Andres went unanswered. So I called him. "What," he grunted. "Hi, Babe! You're still picking me up, right?" I asked sweetly.

Silence.

"Sorry. I can't. I'm really busy buying hats." Click. Now, this was before rideshares, but I got home. I couldn't believe Andres wasn't excited to see me after being apart for a week.

We had been dating since Halloween. I thought I saw fireworks during our first kiss. Looking back it was probably just sparklers from the bottle service at the nightclub we were at. Andres walked into any party like a Carly Simon song. His face was beautifully asymmetrical, like Adrien Brody, and his clear sense of style towered over me at 6'6". Over six feet is my kryptonite. So dating Andres was love at first "how tall are you?"

I liked how Andres made me feel dainty and safe. Especially since Robert (Guy Who's Much Older) used to complain that I was "too tall" in my favorite wedge sandals. Andres represented everything I wanted that I was starved from in my relationship with Robert: youth, confidence, adventure, and the freedom to wear heels.

There was a fire between us. I'd tell complete strangers I was dating my future husband, and I believed it. One night in West Hollywood, we lost each other and he came running up behind me screaming my name. He scooped me up, kissing me, "I love you! I love you! I love you!" He howled into the night. I kissed him deeply. "I love you, too!" I couldn't believe he flaked on my airport pickup.

The month before, I had grabbed him at LAX, thinking he couldn't wait to get his hands on me. But he really couldn't wait to get his hands on a pair of new limited-edition neon orange Jordans. I chauffeured him around until he found them, only to learn he was just going to sell the sneakers online. Instead of getting mad, I admired his side hustle.

Later that night, Andres invited me over and apologized, admitting he was finding

TASTE:	LOOK:	SOUND:	SMELL:	FEEL:
IPAs and vape pens	VIP everywhere	Indie records that are *much* cooler than yours	Eucalyptus from the steam room at the Equinox gym	Like you're back in high school

my Christmas present. It was a necklace with a "G" for my first name and an elephant charm. He remembered I used to call elephants "epi-tints" when I was younger. I thought about the silver beaded bracelet Robert had gotten me for my birthday. An accessory that was so not me, but rather the J. Crew–clad girlfriend he wished I was. While Andres loved me for me, just the way I was.

We never made it to Hawaii. Turns out you can't get on a flight standby on New Year's Eve, even if your roommate's uncle is a pilot. But we had a lovely time celebrating with his friends and their pet pig, Frances Bacon, at a sit-down dinner. The next week I convinced him to wait in line for a free comedy show. "I don't do lines. I *do* lines," he groaned as we waited. That Sunday, we did volunteer work, walking a mutt named Guido. We laughed at how ridiculous it was that this counted as volunteer work. We talked about someday moving in together and getting a mutt of our own.

But Andres kept breaking more promises. While he was never a rebound, I still had baggage and trust issues from being lied to by Robert only a couple months before. Then Andres lost his wallet for the third time since we started dating. "If you're not careful, you'll lose your girlfriend, too," his friends joked. A few days later, he lost me. We ended things sloppily, so we kept making up and breaking up until he moved out of Los Angeles. To this day Andres remains my favorite ex. He is unapologetically and fearlessly himself. When I told him he was The Guy Who's Cooler, he said, "I'm not cool. I just have good taste," which is *such* a cool guy thing to say. Don't be so fixated that The Guy Who's Cooler is cooler than you. You are also cool, and if he can't see that, then is he really that cool?

ARTIST vs. WOKE BRO vs. TOO COOL FOR SCHOOL

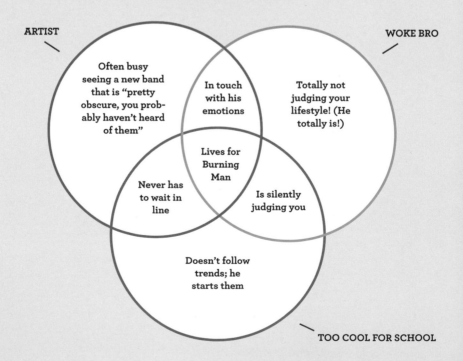

ARTIST

Often busy seeing a new band that is "pretty obscure, you probably haven't heard of them"

In touch with his emotions

WOKE BRO

Totally not judging your lifestyle! (He totally is!)

Lives for Burning Man

Never has to wait in line

Is silently judging you

Doesn't follow trends; he starts them

TOO COOL FOR SCHOOL

BOY BINGO

Good at pool	**Always on "the list," with access to the back room at nightclubs**	**Has a shoe collection** 
Has at least one strategically placed and thoughtful tattoo	**Free space!**	**Knows everyone, and everyone knows him**
Wears glasses, sometimes	**Owns "art"**	**Has at least one plant that is miraculously alive**

IS IT LOVE OR LUST?

Is he perfect?

A Yes! I love every-thing about him! He seriously can do no wrong.

B Of course he's not perfect, he's human. But I accept his flaws. I even find some of his imper-fections sexy.

How much energy do you put into your appearance when you see him?

A A lot! Full hair and makeup, perfectly coordinated outfit. I would die if he ever saw me without my face on and in sweat-pants.

B Are we going somewhere fancy? If not, he's lucky if I shower.

How important is sex?

A Incredibly important. If we don't have sex one night, I assume he's cheating on me or some-thing is very wrong.

B Whenever it happens. I'm satisfied. No complaints here!

How deep are your conversations?

A Pretty surface, TBH.

B Surprisingly deep. I'm attracted to his mind as much as his body.

Do you fight?

A Not really! Remember, he's perfect!

B We get into arguments and on each other's nerves sometimes. But we grow from our fights. It only makes us stronger.

Mostly **A**

You are in lust. You are so swept away with this new and exciting relationship that you are focusing only on the surface and not paying attention to what's inside. Try to take off your rose-colored glasses and see him for who he really is.

Mostly **B**

Sounds like you are actually in love! You are really working at developing a strong relationship. You realize love isn't a fairy tale and are embracing the good with the bad. This has promise!

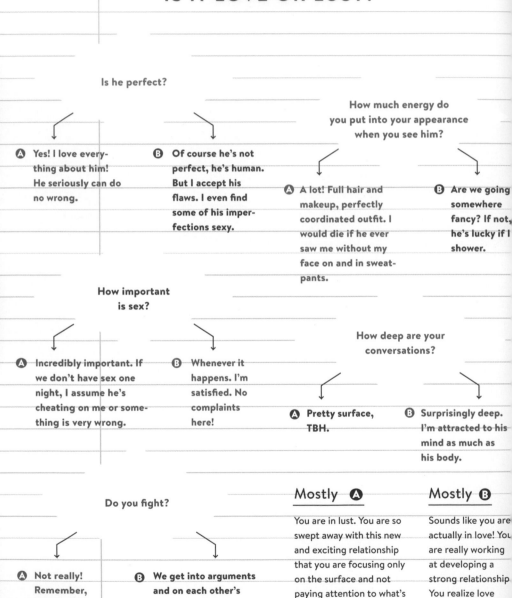

Ask Someone Else

Guy I Dated: Andres, 33, dated for 3 months

I did tell you I'd pick you up and yes, that was a TDM (total dick move). Regarding the guy who's cooler than you, you were the one who ultimately upstaged me. We were at different stages of our lives. Everyone has their ups and downs, and you were on your way up.

Couple: Michelle, 27, & Chris, 48, together 6 months

She is much more talented, thoughtful, intelligent, and kind than I am. She has better taste in music, clothing, literature. She's taught me more about myself, and is the first person I've met who can keep up with me. She leaves me notes, keeps it interesting, makes me feel important, and genuinely likes and is nice to me. I've never met anyone who has undeniably kept my attention from the moment I met her. The cool thing comes into play often more so in my head than in real life. I try not to give advice

because most people are cooler than me, but if I were to I would say enjoy and absorb. If it's the right situation, celebrate it. If it's not, take all you are learning and have learned into the next arena.
—Chris

He is cooler because he is undeniably fearless in matters of life and in love. He is also a comedian and much funnier than me. His coolness only becomes an issue when he began holding me accountable for my bullshit. (My passive-aggressive tendencies were not going to fly in this relationship, which I now find incredibly sexy.) When an issue arises, he calls me up to the plate, so we can communicate effectively to reach a solution. His coolness has encouraged me to practice relaxing and breathing so I can focus in on the task at hand. (Did I mention he is way cooler?) My advice for any girl in their twenties would be to find someone who you can share a mutual respect with. Someone who holds you accountable but is also willing to do the work. Someone who wants to spend time with you but

can give you the freedom to grow. Find someone who is cooler than you because they teach you something important about yourself. Don't settle for anyone who makes you second-guess your worth.
—Michelle

Friend: Gaby, 28

I dated a guy for a month, and I decided I needed to end it because I'm cooler than him. It slowly became clear to me that he was lame. The first sign was when I sent him a selfie of me smoking weed in Jamaica and he responded, "Watch out, you're breaking the law!" and I was like "?!?" Then I started noticing things more. Like he listens to country music and drinks whole milk. But I still haven't ended it because . . . he dropped his phone in a puddle. So, like, I have to wait for that to be resolved.

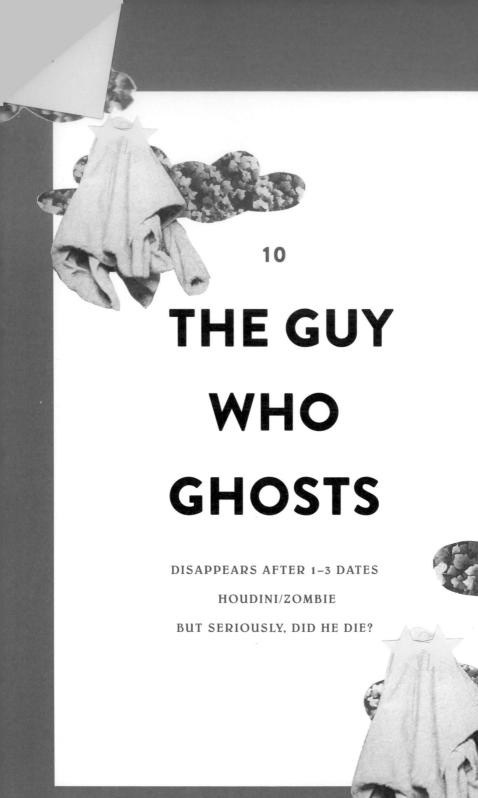

10

THE GUY WHO GHOSTS

DISAPPEARS AFTER 1–3 DATES

HOUDINI/ZOMBIE

BUT SERIOUSLY, DID HE DIE?

"**1** 've never been here before," Sid admitted over candlelight in a cozy leather booth at a tiny French restaurant. I was instantly drawn to his transparency and found myself lost in his big blue eyes.

I was nervous when my friend Perry set us up over email. We each knew what the other looked like (so it wasn't a total blind date; I guess it was more of a visually impaired date?). I knew Sid was tall, Midwestern, and Disney-prince handsome: dashing, strong, and if absolutely necessary, he could totally pull off tights. But I didn't expect our conversation to flow so effortlessly as we tackled everything from our family life to our favorite *Simpsons* episodes.

Then he took me to Yogurtland, which in 2013 was a fantastic date move. Soon we knew more about each other in two hours than I knew about most people in two months. I didn't even look at my phone once for our entire four hour–long date.

On hour four, he kissed me mid-sentence. I hadn't felt this way since I'd first kissed Will (The Guy Who Got Away) in high school. As he leaned in to kiss me again, he whispered, "This is the best date I've ever been on." *Same! Let's hang out forever!* I wanted to scream, but instead, I smirked. "I also had a really nice time."

The next day, he left me a note on my desk at work asking if we could hang out that Saturday. He wanted to show me around where he lived in Calabasas (as in the Kardashians). I had plans that night in Hollywood, but I was determined to make it work.

Contrary to how they make it look on *Keeping Up with the Kardashians*, Calabasas is not close to or even in Los Angeles. But I got there. We watched TV and made out. Sure, the itinerary was much less impressive than our first date, but it didn't matter. I was so into Sid that I would probably find watching paint dry new and exciting as long as I was with him.

And then, I never heard from him. "Should I text him?!" I asked Perry over wine a week later. "Eh, I wouldn't, Gab. I feel like he'd text you if he wanted to see you again." I was so confused. Our last date was totally PG-13. Usually, a guy disappears after sex, not after a steamy makeout session with the anticipation of more.

Deep down I believed he would text me. But days turned into weeks, and there were no more texts, plans, or cute notes on my desk. Soon it became clear what

TASTE:	LOOK:	SOUND:	SMELL:	FEEL:
The most delicious cake you've ever tasted; it was just a dream	A nightmare dressed like a daydream	Crickets chirping	Sulfur	Cold. Do you see dead people?

was happening: something you might call ghosting, but I call Houdini-ing. He was a Houdini who had just pulled off the two-date-disappearing act: magical first date, solid second date, and then—*Poof!* He vanished into thin air!

I kept replaying our last date in my head: What did I do to ruin this?

At the time, I didn't get an explanation, but he didn't really owe me one. It had only been seven emails, one week, one note, and two dates.

Until six years later when I was writing this book. I Facebook-messaged Sid, and to my surprise, he wanted to talk on the phone. Turns out he was in a bad place when we were dating. He meant it when he said it was the best date he ever went on. That wasn't a line. He thought I had

Houdini-ed him due to the unimpressive second date. If I had reached out, he would've absolutely gone on a third date, and who knows what would've developed.

I know. I'm also shocked. Because my advice was going to be: If this happens to you, don't drive yourself crazy. You did absolutely nothing wrong. Accept you've just been Houdini-ed and move on.

But now I'm changing that tune. Houdini-ing/ghosting can go both ways. If deep down you feel like you had a strong connection, sometimes you have to trust your gut. What's the worst that can happen? You already aren't talking to him! Reach out one last time, and if still nothing, accept that it's over so you can make room for a guy who isn't all smoke and mirrors.

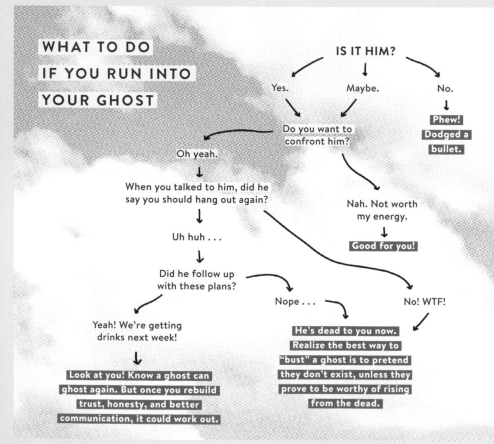

WHAT TO DO IF YOU RUN INTO YOUR GHOST

IS IT HIM?

Yes.   Maybe.   No.

No. → **Phew! Dodged a bullet.**

Do you want to confront him?

Oh yeah.

When you talked to him, did he say you should hang out again?

Uh huh . . .

Did he follow up with these plans?

Nah. Not worth my energy. → **Good for you!**

Yeah! We're getting drinks next week!

Look at you! Know a ghost can ghost again. But once you rebuild trust, honesty, and better communication, it could work out.

Nope . . .   No! WTF!

He's dead to you now. Realize the best way to "bust" a ghost is to pretend they don't exist, unless they prove to be worthy of rising from the dead.

BOY BINGO

Had one of the world's best first dates	Communication went from consistent to nonexistent	Active on social media, but isn't talking to you Joe
Only went on a handful of really good dates	Free space! 	Canceled plans sorry can't make it!
Seriously, did he die?	You reached out to him more than he reached out to you	Your friends are sick of hearing about his disappearing act

IS HE GHOSTING YOU, OR IS HE ACTUALLY DEAD?

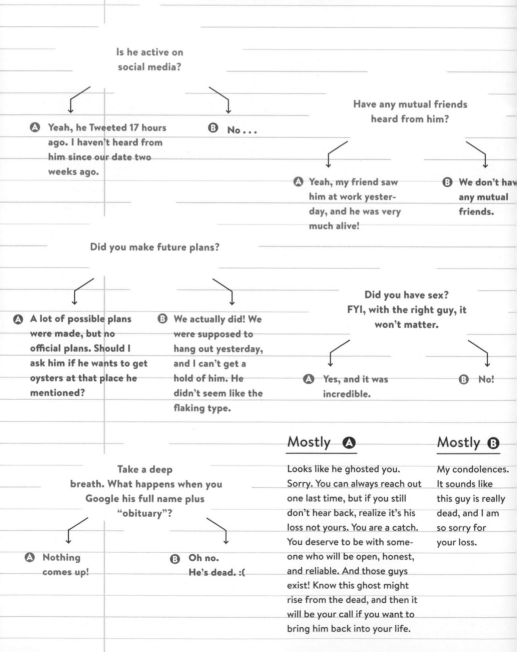

Is he active on social media?

Ⓐ Yeah, he Tweeted 17 hours ago. I haven't heard from him since our date two weeks ago.

Ⓑ No . . .

Have any mutual friends heard from him?

Ⓐ Yeah, my friend saw him at work yester-day, and he was very much alive!

Ⓑ We don't hav any mutual friends.

Did you make future plans?

Ⓐ A lot of possible plans were made, but no official plans. Should I ask him if he wants to get oysters at that place he mentioned?

Ⓑ We actually did! We were supposed to hang out yesterday, and I can't get a hold of him. He didn't seem like the flaking type.

Did you have sex? FYI, with the right guy, it won't matter.

Ⓐ Yes, and it was incredible.

Ⓑ No!

Take a deep breath. What happens when you Google his full name plus "obituary"?

Ⓐ Nothing comes up!

Ⓑ Oh no. He's dead. :(

Mostly Ⓐ

Looks like he ghosted you. Sorry. You can always reach out one last time, but if you still don't hear back, realize it's his loss not yours. You are a catch. You deserve to be with some-one who will be open, honest, and reliable. And those guys exist! Know this ghost might rise from the dead, and then it will be your call if you want to bring him back into your life.

Mostly Ⓑ

My condolences. It sounds like this guy is really dead, and I am so sorry for your loss.

Ask Someone Else

Guy I Dated: Sid, 35, 2 dates

I loved our first date. I liked that we went to Yogurtland. I need to be around people who I can sit and talk with regardless of the setting. I didn't reach out, and you didn't reach out. I just walked away from it, and that has to do with my damage. I was super into you, and it was my own baggage that pulled me out of it. Ghosting has to do with shitty dudes, but the same feeling and insecurities exist on both sides of the gender spectrum. The only thing I would say is you never know what other people's lives are like currently and what baggage they're carrying. If you had hit me up with a couple of texts, we would've gone out again.

Couple: Sandra, 33, & Andrew, 30, together 7 months

We met on Tinder. Started talking the very end of June. Finally met for a date at the end of July. Went out Thursday night for drinks (ended up sleeping together). Then went to dinner again on Saturday. And then lunch on Sunday because he knew I had plans that night and he wanted to see me. So sweet. Then on Monday, he disappeared. I texted him saying I deserve better than him just ignoring me. I also tried calling him. Nothing. Then exactly one week later on the following Monday he texted me saying he was sorry. He told me he freaks out when he gets close to people. He asked if he could take me to dinner and apologize in person. I said yes. We've been seeing each other since. Being ghosted sucks! You instantly wonder what you did wrong. It wasn't you. He is the one with the problem. Not you.

Expert: Erin Darling, cohost of *Ghosted Hunters* podcast

When people ghost they usually think they're doing the "right thing." People ghost to spare the other person's feelings, or to avoid having an awkward conversation. In my opinion, it's better just to bite the bullet and have a brief conversation with some sort of explanation rather than leave the other person hanging. Both parties usually feel better about it in the end. Let the ghost know how you feel. Keep the contact short, casual, and honest, and try not to unleash all your anger or resentment on them. Remember, the goal is to get them to respond, and if you totally lash out, you may regret it later. Don't blame yourself, and don't lose faith. In dating, and in life, follow the golden rule: Treat others the way you'd like to be treated.

11

THE GUY WHO'S TOXIC

YOU KNEW HE
WAS TROUBLE WHEN
HE WALKED IN

my face stings when I think of Chad. I remember when he backhanded me. The sun was still out, but he was blackout drunk. He was cracking himself up, flailing his arms, one of which hit me across the nose. I don't think he meant it, and if you think I'm justifying his actions I'm not. It was more offensive that things were always a joke with Chad. A drunken, hazy comedy act that never left his studio apartment.

I almost never went on a date with Chad. We matched on Tinder, but I declined to meet after knowing we worked in the same industry. But I kept running into Chad and was drawn to his captivating smile, big sweet eyes, and a Macklemore haircut, which was the epitome of cool at the time.

I kept my distance, but Chad would find any excuse to talk to me. My heart raced anytime we crossed paths. Then Chad asked me to grab drinks. I agreed, convincing myself it was the universe and not Chad's persistence that brought us together.

Over Moscow mules, we bonded over dating war stories and our East Coast upbringings. After that date, we spent almost every night together. We shared a mutual obsession with *The Simpsons*. We loved Chex Mix but hated the pretzel pieces. He used to fish them out for me. Little by little, he isolated me from my friends, telling me I was his best friend, and he was the only friend I ever needed.

Then, I noticed he was buying a new handle of Smirnoff every other day from CVS. But it was the holidays, so I just told myself he was a fun guy. We'd stay up nights having deep conversations, dissecting everything from human behavior to our favorite literature. We'd look out at the city of stars from his roof. He'd tell me we could conquer this town as long as we were together. I believed him.

One day he pinched the fat slipping over my skinny jeans. "Getting comfortable?" He knew the answer. Anytime I was fearlessly me, he'd shake his head. "I wish I could refine your presence." One day out of nowhere, he whispered, "I can't wait until you turn 30 and realize you aren't funny." I was 26.

Then it got physical. Prior to the smack, he kicked me off his bed. I landed on my elbow and had to keep it in a sling for a week. Both times he was drunk; both times he was careless; both times he "didn't mean it." Like a little boy playing too rough with the family cat.

TASTE:	LOOK:	SOUND:	SMELL:	FEEL:
On-sale sushi you know will give you food poisoning the next day	Your parents won't approve	The whoop of a fire alarm	Perfume . . . wait, that's not your scent . . .	You can't do better

I never saw this behavior as abusive because I didn't look like the battered girlfriend I saw in movies. He never (purposely) hit me, and I never hid a black eye with concealer. His abuse was subtle but manipulative. Like the night he held my face and looked deep into my eyes as Billy Joel's "She's Always a Woman" played. "You're my woman. You're my best friend. You're my wife!" No one had ever called me their wife before. Most guys didn't even call me back. The next day he was short with me. What had I done since last night to make him not love me anymore?

"Okay, Nicole Brown Simpson," my best friend, Kris, said when I told her what was happening. I realized I needed to get out before it got worse.

One night at the Rusty Mullet, a bar in Hollywood that lives up to its name, Chad got into an argument with a stranger about something that didn't matter. Taylor Swift's "Mean" came on. It was a sign. For the first time, I saw Chad as who he really was: "mean and a liar and pathetic. And alone in life and mean."

It was hard to find the right time to end things. So I broke up with him the day before Valentine's Day. I forgot about my abusive ex for a while. But triggers will spark my memory: pretzel pieces in Chex Mix, certain *Simpsons* episodes, anytime I see a Macklemore haircut in the liquor section at CVS. I almost left this story out because I wanted to forget it. Unfortunately, this is a reality of dating. You might feel you can't get out of an abusive relationship because he convinces you that you can't do better. I'm here to tell you from the other side that it's not true. It's never true.

Red Flags and the Excuses We Make for Them

▶ **UNPREDICTABLE**

"Every day's an adventure!"

Sounds like every day is a heartache. There are stable guys out there who will not take their issues out on you. I promise.

▶ **CONTROLLING**

"He just wants me to be my best self!"

If he wants you to be your best self, he will embrace your flaws and offer solutions to problems, not only criticism.

▶ **ALWAYS DRUNK**

"He's just a fun guy!"

This sounds like a drinking problem. If it is, the only way he's going to change his ways is if he wants to.

▶ **IGNORES YOU**

"He's just teaching me independence."

No, this is actually rude. Unless there is a valid excuse for why he's ignoring you, this is manipulative and cruel, and you deserve better.

▶ **NEEDY**

"Aw, he can't live without me."

This is actually a sign of codependency. If he can't take care of himself and expects you to do everything for him, this is not a partnership. Set boundaries and keep them.

▶ **LACK OF COMMUNICATION**

"Honestly, we're so close, we don't even need to talk."

Actually, communication is the cornerstone of any relationship. It's key. You need to talk. Your voice should be heard, especially when something is bothering you.

▶ **IMPORTANT PEOPLE IN YOUR LIFE DON'T LIKE HIM**

"They're just jealous!"

They're actually not! Your friends and family want the best for you, always. I can't tell you how many times my friends and family were right about something I didn't want to believe was true.

BOY BINGO

Gaslights	Manipulates	Mean

Has drinking and/ or substance abuse problem	**Free space!**	**Cheats**

Always blames you	**Controlling**	**Isolates you from your friends and family**

Quiz

ARE YOU IN AN ABUSIVE RELATIONSHIP?

What does he think about people in your life who are important to you?

A He hates them all, but he also brought up some good points about my best friend. She really *is* jealous!

B He gets along well with them!

What do you do when you hang out?

A We normally are just with each other. We rarely hang out with other people unless we absolutely have to. But we also don't like most people!

B Depends what's goin on! Sometimes we li to chill at home, but we're both social an love to hang out wit each other's friends

If you don't text or call him back immediately, what happens?

A He'll text more. Freak out. Call me. But he's right, I really should be paying attention to my phone, even when I'm doing other things. What if it was an emergency?!

B Nothing. He knows and respects that I have a life outside of our relationship.

How does he feel about your hopes and dreams?

A He'll listen, but he also doesn't think they're realistic. I get it. I should use my time to do something more attainable.

B He's supportive. He helps me when I need it but gives me space when I don't.

Do you trust him?

A Not entirely. There were a couple of lies I caught him in, but he promises it will never happen again. I want to believe him, but deep down I'm scared he will do it again.

B 100 percent. We have a very honest and trusting relationship. Our communication is excellent.

Mostly **A**

There are a lot of red flags you seem to be ignoring. You may want to consider speaking with friends, family, or a licensed therapist about this situation. If you would like to reach out but do not know who to call, call the National Domestic Violence Hotline (1-800-799-7233) or National Sexual Assault Hotline (1-800-656-4673).

Mostly **B**

He sounds overall supportive. But if you answered A for any of these questions, don't ignore that. Those are signs of an abusive rela tionship. You may want to consider speaking with friends, family, or licensed therapist abou this situation.

Ask Someone Else

Friend: Taylor, 27

I didn't realize I was in an abusive relationship. My excuse was, "He's young. Let me fix him. He will learn!" But no matter how many times I spelled things out—he wouldn't change. There were so many red flags! He tried to control what I wore, what I did on social media. He didn't let me have a social life. He was always accusing me of cheating. He'd go through my phone. My advice on getting over it is to go on dates! Stay busy! But it's fine to take naps and watch Netflix, too. Just do things that make you happy. And cry. It's okay to cry. Deleting photos and videos, and blocking him was crucial for me, too. Look at your situation and ask yourself, "Is this how I want to live for the rest of my life?" If the answer is no, get out. It's easier said than done, but there are more than 7.5 billion people on Earth. He's not the one. Or, as Cristina Yang from *Grey's Anatomy* would say, "He is not the sun. You are."

Expert: John Kim, LMFT, the Angry Therapist, author of *I Used to Be a Miserable F*ck*

If you're in an abusive relationship, you need to make a plan to get out safely. But you shouldn't do it alone. Get support from friends and family. You may not want to tell anyone due to shame in being in something abusive, but hiding it will only create your own prison. A few red flags to look out for: character assassination; uncontrollable anger and outbursts that lead to apologizing but then happening again, and this turning into a pattern; and growing controlling behavior. Enough is enough when there is no change.

Expert: Padua Eaton, founder of mental health charity Do the Thing UK

I didn't realize I was in an abusive relationship until afterward. I was only 16. His behavior was controlling but indirect. For example, he would tell me he didn't like something but say, "It's your life. You can do what you want." Then, if I went and did that thing he would punish me by withdrawing and not talking to me. This manipulation through negative reinforcement is not okay. He would also gaslight me. If you start questioning your own sanity, it's time to get out. Every time they hurt you, write it down. Tell your friends about their behavior; get reassurance that these behaviors are wrong. I recommend having therapy as well (or at least set something up for when you leave the relationship). You will be able to uncover more of the manipulation that way, and you'll have that support when you walk away.

12

THE GUY WHO'S NOT YOUR BOYFRIEND

UNAVAILABLE

"NOT INTO LABELS"

COMMITMENT ISSUES

adam and I were attempting to make Blue Apron's Maple-Mustard Roasted Chicken. "I thought you said you knew how to cook," he laughed as I struggled to cut the sweet potato wedges. "I do! But the Italian way, which means I make it up as I go along!" He kissed me. "You're adorable," he whispered.

I was so deeply in love with Adam, which was weird because he wasn't my boyfriend. We had been dating for six months and did all the things couples do, like trying meal kits (his idea) or exploring new restaurants (my idea). Adam was everything I wanted in a boyfriend. He was smart, patient, passionate, and funny.

We ended up burning the chicken and ordering a pizza. This was symbolic of us. We had everything to create the perfect relationship, but we couldn't make it work. Our baggage from past relationships haunted us. Adam broke up with his last serious girlfriend a week before we met. I had major trust issues from ending things with Chad (The Guy Who's Toxic) a month earlier. I didn't believe Adam when he said he wasn't ready to be my boyfriend. All I heard was "not your boyfriend" and assumed he was seeing other women. Eventually, this ate away at our relationship.

I changed his name in my phone to "Not Your Boyfriend," but that didn't stop me from drunk texting him. When I finally stopped, he started reaching out to me. I told him he should talk to a therapist about his commitment issues, and he did.

One day he left a package at my door of two dozen red roses, pictures of us, my favorite sweatshirt of his he'd never let me take home, and a note asking me to call. So I did. He told me he was ready to be my boyfriend. I told him I knew he only wanted me because he couldn't have me. Also, red roses?! How generic. How did he not know my favorite flower was white lilies? (I feel like a brat even typing that.)

But he still kept showing up. Supporting me at my comedy shows with my favorite dessert (banana pudding), and an ear to listen to how I thought it went. I should've appreciated this, but I was still hurt from being dangled around for months. Then he stopped showing up. So I started reaching out, until I learned he was in a new relationship. This broke me. But I also knew I had to let him go for good this time.

TASTE:	LOOK:	SOUND:	SMELL:	FEEL:
Tequila shot, hard to swallow but makes you feel warm inside	Looks like your boyfriend, especially to everyone else	A record scratching	Coffee brewing	Anxious, uncertain, conflicted— basically all the feelings!

We hadn't talked for five years when I was writing this. I reached out to him on Facebook, assuming my message would go unanswered. To my surprise, he called me. He's married now, and I'm happy for him. He told me he saw my best friend, Kris, on the street and told the friend he was with, "That's my ex-girlfriend's best friend." I almost dropped my iPhone. "I'm sorry, what did you call me? Your *ex-girlfriend*?!" We shared a laugh.

He explained he really did care about me, and he was never seeing other women when we were together. "I was finally ready to commit to you when I asked you to be my girlfriend. I realized I was missing out on something amazing because of fear." Finally, the words I longed to hear—five years too late. I told my parents about Adam over Korean BBQ. "Let me get this straight. He had a good job, really liked you, was always honest with you, and when he finally committed to you, you turned him down?" my dad said, biting into a shrimp. "Well, you really messed this one up, didn't you?" He laughed. I took a sip of my beer. My dad was right.

It takes two people to be in a relationship. You both have to decide if you can wait, have trust, and be on the same page. And when it is meant to be, it just happens, and it isn't a battle. Being in a relationship is like cooking: You need all the right ingredients, a recipe, and time for it to turn out just right.

NOT YOUR BOYFRIEND vs. NOT THAT INTO YOU

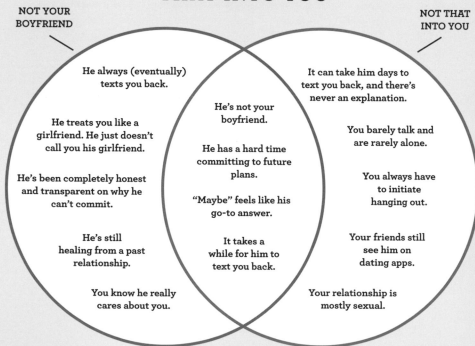

NOT YOUR BOYFRIEND

He always (eventually) texts you back.

He treats you like a girlfriend. He just doesn't call you his girlfriend.

He's been completely honest and transparent on why he can't commit.

He's still healing from a past relationship.

You know he really cares about you.

He's not your boyfriend.

He has a hard time committing to future plans.

"Maybe" feels like his go-to answer.

It takes a while for him to text you back.

NOT THAT INTO YOU

It can take him days to text you back, and there's never an explanation.

You barely talk and are rarely alone.

You always have to initiate hanging out.

Your friends still see him on dating apps.

Your relationship is mostly sexual.

BOY BINGO

Labels scare him 	**His ex is still very much a part of his life**	**You're not his girlfriend**
He recently got out of a very serious relationship	**Free space!** 	**You've been dating for at least three months, and he still won't define the relationship**
Not in therapy	**Home is whenever you're with him**	**You think he's the one**

WILL YOUR UNAVAILABLE GUY SOMEDAY BE AVAILABLE TO YOU?

How is your communication?

Ⓐ Incredible. We can talk about almost anything. I feel like he really hears and understands me.

Ⓑ Not great. I don't think he understands how hurt I am that he won't commit to me.

Is there another woman?

Ⓐ No, and I believe him. But of course, I can't help but wonder if maybe there is, that would explain why he can't commit!

Ⓑ I'm almost positive there's someone else.

Aside from the lack of title, how does he treat you?

Ⓐ Like a girlfriend—down to the respect, the attention, and the partnership.

Ⓑ I never feel like a priority.

What do your friends think?

Ⓐ They like him, but they don't like seeing me this hurt.

Ⓑ They hate him. They don't think there's a future.

What does your gut say?

Ⓐ When you know you know, right? Deep down I feel like he is the one, and I should be patient.

Ⓑ Something is off. Maybe I shouldn't wait around to find out.

Mostly Ⓐ

It's going to be tough. If you have excellent communication, are treated as equal, and it feels like deep down this is your person, be patient. It could work out.

Mostly Ⓑ

It doesn't seem like this guy is giving you the love and respect you deserve. Honestly, a title might not change that. And you are title-worthy! He should want everyone to know you are his! You're the best Don't waste any more time Remember, love the thing that loves you back.

Ask Someone Else

Guy I Dated: Adam, 33, dated for 6 months

You were completely justified in the way you felt. You were ready for the title sooner than I was, and that's a very vulnerable place to be, especially when you really like someone and you're not sure it's reciprocated. You thinking "he only wants what he can't have and it's not actually real" is absolutely fair. I would say that's the case 99 percent of the time. Unfortunately, it took you cutting the cord for me to get to the place of "what am I so worried about?" And by then it was too late. Even though this might have been an exception to the rule, that doesn't mean it would've worked out in the end. Dating is essentially emotional gambling. In the end, you just have to trust yourself, listen to that inner true and honest part of you and what you think to be true for the other person. We both knew we were on different pages but wanted it to work out, so we kept it going until we hit that emotional crossroads and had to pick a path.

Couple: Becca, 28, & Alex, 35, together for 7 years

What we both thought would be a one-night stand ended up turning into a seven-year relationship. From that moment on, it was pretty obvious we were meant to be. Or at least it was to me (Becca). It was a classic case of commitment phobia. I was heartbroken but totally aware that he was being an idiot. So I did what any self-assured, independent woman would do: date other people and then go home and cry in my pillow. To my fortune, Alex couldn't stand the fact that I went out with anyone else. We became official and Alex moved in a week later. Know your worth! Don't put up with the bullshit. There would be times I didn't want to wait up until 2 a.m., drink cheap tequila, and pretend like I lived in eyeliner. Sometimes I'd look at myself and be like, why am I doing this for a boy?! (It was because I was madly in love with him, but still!)

Expert: Bruna Nessif, CPC, ELI-MP, author of *Let That Shit Go*

The issue with holding out for someone who won't commit to you is that you're continuously making a choice to stall your life based on the hope that something will change, rather than finding acceptance in what actually is, and this can lead to disappointment, resentment, and unreachable expectations. Many of us do this, because we convince ourselves we're "fighting for love," but unconditional love is given freely and abundantly. Believe you deserve more than someone who's only willing to give you some-timey-halfway love. I wish I could tell my younger self this exact thing. I also wish I could tell her that it's not my responsibility to fix people, and that it's not my job to prove I'm worth loving, because those who actually love me would never make me question where I stand or whether or not I'm worthy of their time.

13

THE GUY YOU CAN'T REMEMBER

MIKE? OR WAS IT MATT?

BASIC BRO

SERIOUSLY, WHAT WAS
HIS NAME?!

Our first date was at one of "the most romantic spots in Los Angeles," according to this bar's Yelp page. I was 26, and we met when I was drunk-swiping on JSwipe (Jewish Tinder). While I'm not a chosen one, I was hoping someone would choose me. Then suddenly, mazel tov! A match!

He had a dimpled smile, a great body, and lived only one mile away? My type physically *and* geographically? Sure, his pictures were a little basic, like that shot of him holding a kid that his bio assured me was not his. But it felt promising that our conversation quickly moved from messenger to first date plans.

I was relieved to discover that he actually looked like his photos. When I extended my hand to introduce myself, he pulled me in for a hug. "We actually met before," he whispered. My face grew red as I looked into his eyes. I couldn't place him.

"Erica's pool party. I'm her neighbor," he smiled. I squinted in the dim chandelier lighting. I did remember him and his body glistening in the late June sun like a Jewish Adonis. We flirted, then went our separate ways. I assumed I'd see him again. But the days got chillier, and we didn't cross paths. I began to wonder if we had really met or if he was just a figment of my poolside Prosecco-induced imagination.

At first, I was giddy to find out he was real! Then I got weirded out. We had been talking for about a week now. Why didn't he mention he recognized me? Did he think I wouldn't go on this date had I known we'd met before? Then I noticed the flex of his forearm as he dipped a carrot into a bowl of hummus.

Aside from that somewhat creepy setback, the date was fine, until he revealed, "I've been doing CrossFit for about two years now. There's a great sense of community; it just makes me feel part of something. Yesterday I lifted 250 pounds. Can you believe that?! 250 pounds?!"

I felt as dry as the barely touched pita chips on our hummus platter. I didn't need to hear *how* he looked like a Greek god; I just needed him to look like one. Was it now my turn to reveal how I looked like this? I wanted to tell him about my journey with wearing makeup: "I've been going to Sephora since high school. There's a great sense of community with the Sephora Beauty Insiders program; it just makes me feel part of something! Yesterday I spent 250 dollars there. Can you believe that?! 250 dollars to make my face look like I don't need makeup?!"

I left this date unable to tell you what he did for a living, how many siblings he had, or what his favorite food was. The

TASTE:	LOOK:	SOUND:	SMELL:	FEEL:
Mayonnaise	Has eyes	The hum of a football game on TV	Stale beer	Indifferent

conversation was dull. We barely had common ground, aside from the literal common ground of being neighbors. But I never forgot how much he loved CrossFit.

We didn't go on another date. I forgot about this CrossFit cutie until I ran into him at a local coffee shop while I was writing this book. We made small talk, and as I looked into his brown (?) eyes, I realized something. Just like I couldn't place him on our first date, for the life of me I couldn't remember his name. I felt like a mom trying to name that actor from that movie.

So I emailed my friend Erica to see if she could help. She told me his name was Sam. Of course! Sam! I knew that. She also gave me his last name but was unsure of the spelling. And then the strangest thing happened. I couldn't find him anywhere online. Maybe the Internet forgot him, too. Or he blocked me on everything.

Then I remembered something. My old roommate Sydney knew him, too! She never forgot that one time I left the kitchen a mess. Surely she'd remember his name. And she did! Finally, I found him on Facebook and sent him a direct message. I think the advice for The Guy You Can't Remember goes both ways. There are plenty of fish in the sea and plenty of guys holding up fish in the sea of dating app profile pics. Focus on what makes you unique, and soon you will hook your person.

What to Do When You Forget a Date's Name

You realize you have no idea what your date's name is.

Introduce yourself to the bartender/waiter, so your date will have to introduce himself.

He's not friendly? Show him your driver's license photo because it's so embarrassing, and ask to see his!

He doesn't drive? Ask what his handle is on whichever social media platform you don't follow him on.

He's not on social media? When the bill comes, insist on splitting it and glance at his card/receipt.

Did he pay in cash? Er, tell him you want to email a funny article and ask for his email.

His email isn't his name? Okay, ask him how he spells his name.

He says "like it sounds"? Start calling him "Bro," "Dude," or "Man."

He asked you to stop? Tell him you can analyze handwriting. Have him print his full name.

He can't spell his name? Run!

BOY BINGO

Wears shirts most of the time	**Has facial hair on occasion**	**Likes sports**
Owns more than one baseball hat	**Free space!** 	**You have no idea what color his eyes are**
Don't know his full name Tom	**He went to college; you just don't know where**	**He has a major crush on Tom Brady. Or was it Derek Jeter? LeBron James?**

Quiz

ARE YOU DATING A GUY YOU'LL PROBABLY FORGET?

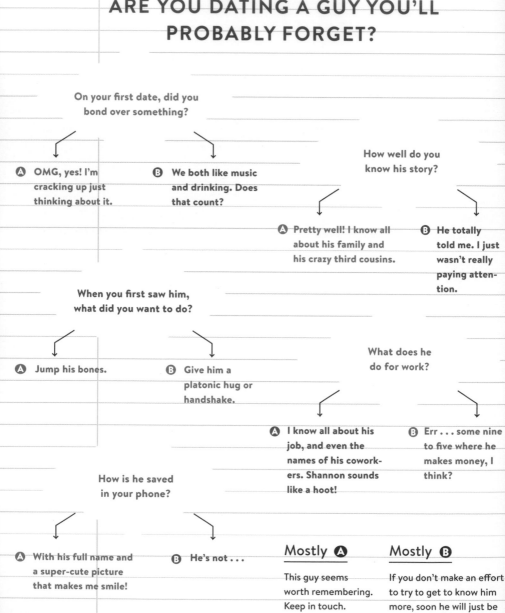

On your first date, did you bond over something?

Ⓐ OMG, yes! I'm cracking up just thinking about it.

Ⓑ We both like music and drinking. Does that count?

How well do you know his story?

Ⓐ Pretty well! I know all about his family and his crazy third cousins.

Ⓑ He totally told me. I just wasn't really paying attention.

When you first saw him, what did you want to do?

Ⓐ Jump his bones.

Ⓑ Give him a platonic hug or handshake.

What does he do for work?

Ⓐ I know all about his job, and even the names of his coworkers. Shannon sounds like a hoot!

Ⓑ Err . . . some nine to five where he makes money, I think?

How is he saved in your phone?

Ⓐ With his full name and a super-cute picture that makes me smile!

Ⓑ He's not . . .

Mostly Ⓐ

This guy seems worth remembering. Keep in touch.

Mostly Ⓑ

If you don't make an effort to try to get to know him more, soon he will just be somebody that you used to know.

Ask Someone Else

Guy I Dated: Sam, 32, 1 date

It wasn't 250 pounds, it was 265 pounds. Also, my eyes are green.

Couple: Vanessa, 34, & James 34, together 10 years

We met New Year's Eve, I (James) was in a stage in my life where I was dating a lot. I even brought a date to this New Year's party but ditched her. Vanessa and I made out, but she pushed me away. I found out we had actually met ten years before. I felt bad about how I acted, so I found her on Facebook and asked her out to dinner. We went out and the rest is history. Our advice for the guy or girl you can't remember is to give them another chance, especially if he is persistent and sincere. What sealed the deal for both of us is we had mutual friends who assured Vanessa that I was actually a great guy. So always check references when dating. My wife only gave me a second shot because I was open, honest, and persistent. She knew, or at least believed, that I was making her a priority, and I was.

Expert: Jen Glantz, professional bridesmaid, @jenglantz

One of the weird things I used to do when I was dating was I would save my date's name in my phone with an adjective so I would remember them. Like "Joe Hockey Player with Brown Hair" or "Alex Lower East Side." I'd even add a photo to their contact so I could keep all my dates straight. When I'm working as a professional bridesmaid, that's even more challenging. I have a fake name, *and* I have to remember everyone else's names! I get around remembering everyone's names by awkwardly going out of the way to avoid saying other people's names. I'll introduce someone I'm with first, so the person will have to say their name. Or I'll do the social media trick and ask to add that person on Facebook so I can see their name. It's hard!

14

THE GUY WHO'S A ONE-NIGHT STAND

"I SWEAR I NEVER DO THIS!"

BOYFRIEND FOR THE NIGHT

HIT IT AND QUIT IT

1 woke up in Peter's arms happy. He looked like Jeremy Sisto, which, as a *Clueless*–obsessed millennial, was hard to resist. Yet I managed to not have sex with him the night prior. Go me! But he looked so handsome, with his tousled hair and hazel eyes sparkling in the morning light, I couldn't help myself. Is it a one-night stand, if it's the next morning? I told myself absolutely not.

I'd met Peter the night prior at a sports bar with my best friend, Lesley, when he and his equally tall brother challenged us to a game of beer pong. They destroyed us and bought us a pitcher of beer as a consolation prize. Over Bud Light, we learned they used to play basketball professionally. I connected with Peter. I found it fascinating that he was single and not on any dating apps, which was unusual in 2014. I found it even more fascinating that he was also a John Mayer fan, which was unusual since Mayer's infamous 2010 *Playboy* interview.

At last call, Peter asked me if I wanted to go to his place. Now, I don't typically go home with guys I just met at bars. But for some reason, and maybe it was that last shot of Jägermeister, I decided to go home with this handsome stranger.

The more I found out about Peter, the more I liked him. He had a vinyl player, was teaching himself French, and liked to cook. Then I saw the framed Nickelback tickets. Not like nosebleed "Hey, wouldn't it be funny if we went to a Nickelback concert" tickets. Like, front row center tickets. As I was writing this, I wondered if Nickelback was really that bad. So I listened to "How You Remind Me," and I could barely get through the first verse without covering my ears. And that's their most popular song. I can't imagine sitting through a whole concert of their music.

The next morning I gave Peter my number. He promised to call and future plans were thrown around. I was positive he'd be blowing up my phone. But a couple hours later as I dished the details with Lesley over egg-white scrambles . . . there still wasn't a text.

Lesley assured me he'd text. She saw the fireworks. So I went about my Sunday, checking my phone more than usual. He wrote my number down instead of putting it in his phone. What if he wrote it wrong? Or what if I was so hungover that I gave him the wrong number?

TASTE:	LOOK:	SOUND:	SMELL:	FEEL:
Jägermeister	Stride of pride	Chime! Your shared ride is here!	Dry shampoo	Empowered

Feeling powerless, I decided to follow him on Twitter, hoping it would be a nudge. Then I looked him up on Facebook and saw we had a mutual friend. I asked her about him, and she admitted they dated once, but he was "too clingy." That's weird. Maybe he's playing it cool.

A week passed until finally: *Bing!* It was him with an excuse of why there was a delay. He said last Saturday was "fantastic." Wouldn't you want "fantastic" again? Maybe even date "fantastic?" "All good. Let's do it again sometime," I texted back. Nothing. A day passed. Still nothing, so I added, "Or not." And . . . nothing.

Then I got a voicemail. A one-minute-and-forty-one-second voicemail from Peter. In my delusional state, I assumed he was asking me out to dinner. He seemed old-fashioned (hello, vinyl record player).

Instead, he told me he was not that into me for one minute and forty-one seconds. With lines like, "I think you're a fun, cool human being," and "If I was ten years younger, we'd probably date for a while." And then, "I could see after spending a long night with you that we weren't quite right for each other."

Ouch.

One-night stands are just as liberating as they are problematic. Not because the guy will think you're slutty for sleeping with him after one date. If he does, f*ck him! Wait, never mind. You already did that. When you sleep with someone you just met, you don't know that person well enough. Sometimes this leads to a second date; sometimes you learn you're dating a misogynist and it ends there. But if you're really lucky, it ends with a voicemail.

What's in Your Purse?! (In Case You Get Lucky)

- ☐ Condoms: Always practice safe sex, especially with strangers!

- ☐ Hair ties, bobby pins, comb, and dry shampoo: To transform your JBF (just been f*cked) hair into a sleek ponytail or bun

- ☐ Wisps and/or Listerine strips: For breath that's so fresh and so clean

- ☐ Make-up wipes: To wipe off the mascara running down your face

- ☐ Perfume sample: It's not your scent, but it works when you can't shower

- ☐ Mini deodorant: The people in your rideshare will thank you

- ☐ Sunglasses: "I'm not hungover; *you're* hungover"

BOY BINGO

Had sex after knowing each other for less than 24 hours	**No second date**	**Did the walk of shame/stride of pride out of his apartment**
Never have to see him again	**Free space!** 	**Not really compatible outside of the bedroom**
You did something embarrassing and would be fine if you never saw him again	**Sex was fine**	**He's essentially a stranger** TIM?

Quiz

SHOULD YOU TURN YOUR ONE-NIGHT STAND INTO A TWO-NIGHT STAND?

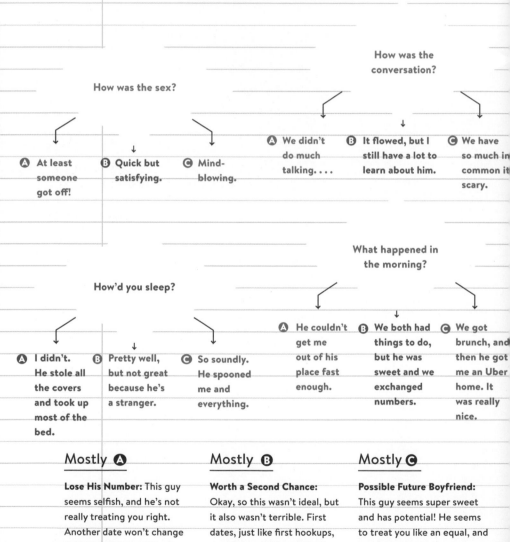

How was the sex?

A At least someone got off!

B Quick but satisfying.

C Mind-blowing.

How was the conversation?

A We didn't do much talking....

B It flowed, but I still have a lot to learn about him.

C We have so much in common it scary.

How'd you sleep?

A I didn't. He stole all the covers and took up most of the bed.

B Pretty well, but not great because he's a stranger.

C So soundly. He spooned me and everything.

What happened in the morning?

A He couldn't get me out of his place fast enough.

B We both had things to do, but he was sweet and we exchanged numbers.

C We got brunch, and then he got me an Uber home. It was really nice.

Mostly **A**

Lose His Number: This guy seems selfish, and he's not really treating you right. Another date won't change that. Unless he makes some changes, I think it's safe to say, "Thank you. Next!" to this one.

Mostly **B**

Worth a Second Chance: Okay, so this wasn't ideal, but it also wasn't terrible. First dates, just like first hookups, can be incredibly awkward. There seems to be some potential here. It might be worth it to have a second date, you know, outside the bedroom.

Mostly **C**

Possible Future Boyfriend: This guy seems super sweet and has potential! He seems to treat you like an equal, and you have a lot in common. How exciting!

Ask Someone Else

Guy I Dated: Peter, 40, 1 night

I have no desire to defend Nickelback (and wouldn't have you change the story because I recognize that it's something of a touchstone here), but I will mention that I was a music writer at the time and went to all sorts of shows! Anyway, I appreciate you reaching out about this and wish you all the best with the book! I don't know that I'd have any advice for the potential dater because I think your closing argument is a good one.

Couple: Lyssa 31, & Phil 32, together 7 years

Our first date was an agreement to have sex. We both wanted to have adventures. Neither of us wanted to have a relationship or were interested emotionally, but seven years later, here we are. When we started, it was effortless. We felt like we had stumbled onto something that was so simple to get into, and we didn't want to leave. Communication is the most important thing, taking responsibility for your own feelings that are developing. Checking in with yourself. Is this turning into feelings? When a relationship starts with the body, knowing your emotional boundaries is key. Keep tabs on yourself and maintain healthy boundaries.

Expert: Daliya Karnofsky, dating coach, host of *Not Your Therapist* podcast

If the one-night stand was fun, let the person know that you had a great time and you'd love to do it again. No need to reach out more after that. If they had a good time, similar to a first date, they'll reach out again.

The forming of any relationship depends on timing and chemistry, and if one of those isn't lined up, it won't grow into a long-term relationship. You can't "destroy a potential future relationship."

Generally, if a relationship is what you want, I recommend not sleeping with someone for at least a few dates. Sleeping together is going to change how you feel about each other, for better or worse. If it's amazing it could make you like each other more than you would have otherwise, and then you'll potentially get into a not-great relationship because of the super sex. If it's disastrous, it could ruin the chances of the relationship going any further, even if the two of you are super compatible. If you have a one-night stand and want to build something, consider not sleeping with them again until you know their personality and how you feel about them.

Overall, I think if two people are a good fit, sleeping together or not won't mess it up. But I do think you should wait to clarify feelings and what you want without the relationship being clouded by the immediate intimacy of sex. But also, it's your twenties! Have sex and mess things up! You're supposed to! How else will you learn what you like and want? Have some adventures, but make sure to take care of yourself.

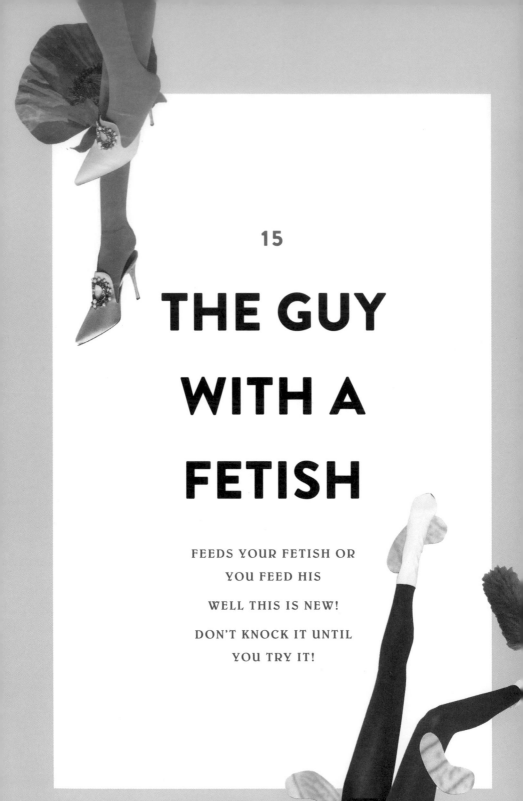

15

THE GUY WITH A FETISH

FEEDS YOUR FETISH OR
YOU FEED HIS

WELL THIS IS NEW!

DON'T KNOCK IT UNTIL
YOU TRY IT!

I knew there was something special about "Andrew, 31" on our first date, despite meeting him on a dating app. The obvious was his British accent. Sure, his V-necks were deeper than mine, but then he'd say "shed-dju-all" or "lit-tra-lee," and I would literally melt into the leather booth right on schedule.

Over shoestring fries, I learned he was divorced. I asked if they still kept in touch, and he said they recently reunited and discovered that they were both into "kinky stuff."

Well. I majored in journalism, so this date was not going to end until I found out exactly what type of kinky stuff. "Do you have a red room? Is it bondage? Role-play?" I asked.

Then gently . . .

"Foot. Stuff?"

He nodded. I bit into a shoestring fry. *Is that why he ordered these?*

At that point, my knowledge of foot fetishes began and ended with a *Sex and the City* episode where Charlotte (the innocent one) notices a shoe salesman getting aroused watching her try on shoes. I had to learn more.

Andrew, 31, told me that growing up he went to a brothel where there was a hallway of feet posing in windows. I asked him if he had a foot type, and he said clean and manicured. How could he really be into feet if he didn't know that it was called a pedicure?

We kept chatting after the date. I was into him because he texted me back. Maybe this could work! One day, I told him I was picking out an outfit, and he asked for a picture, requesting "Don't forget the shoes." I sent him a shot of my floral dress and pink strappy stilettos, holding my breath as I hit send. I'd never sent a nude photo (with my face in it) before, but somehow this felt dirtier. Not because I was judging what gets someone off (as long as it happens between two consenting adults).

What felt shameful was the realization that this was leading to me giving up something: my "foot-gin-ity." There was a time I wanted to save my virginity for marriage. So maybe I should save *something* for marriage, like my feet?

Then, I heard the words of my Grandma Antoinette in my head: "Don't knock it until you try it, Gabriella!" Sure, she was referring to her pasta "fazool," but maybe that was the key to finding love. Being more open-minded in the bedroom? We were both looking for soulmates, just, like, completely different types of souls/soles.

TASTE:	LOOK:	SOUND:	SMELL:	FEEL:
Hard to swallow at first	Like he has a secret	"Love Me Like You Do" by Ellie Goulding	Leather	Out of your comfort zone

Andrew, 31, and I went on a couple of dates until I felt ready. I decided to get a pedicure for the big night. After all, he said he liked "clean manicured (pedicured) feet." It was the least I could do. I went with a violet shade, and I am NOT making this up, the color was called "all access pass."

I splurged on the $60 spa pedicure, where they take off all your dead skin. But while the pedicurist was scraping at the bottom of my foot, I kept getting ticklish. If I couldn't sit still during a spa pedicure, how was I going to lose my foot-gin-ity?

Getting ready for my date, I focused exclusively on my shoes.

Heels?

No, that would ruin my pedicure.

Open toe shoes?

Nah, too slutty.

So, I settled on ankle boots, with a sock, so there was more to take off. Mom and Dad, this would be a good place to stop reading.

Back at his place, he went down on me, and then downer. Slowly removing my boots, then my socks. He did not have sex with my feet. He just kind of sucked on them. I had to hold my breath so I wouldn't laugh. It felt like he was nibbling the dead skin off, like I imagine those tiny fish at spas do. Honestly, this whole experience was shocking. *How was there still dead skin on my $60 spa-pedicured feet?!*

I stopped seeing Andrew, 31, after this night. Not because of the foot thing. More because he lived in Santa Monica, and I lived in West Hollywood, and that's at least an hour commute on a good day. Brutal, right? But I learned a valuable lesson: Never spend $60 on a spa pedicure for a guy you just met on a dating app. Do that for yourself.

BOY BINGO

Always up for an adventure	**Can tell he has a secret**	**Bored by missionary sex**
Enjoys props in the bedroom	**Free space!** 	**Kink or fetish is a little out of your comfort zone, but you're willing to give it a try**
Incredibly sexy	**You've been rewatching or rereading *Fifty Shades of Grey* since you started hanging out**	**You're curious— you're very curious**

CAN YOU DATE A GUY WITH A FETISH?

Is your partner also willing to explore what turns you on?

A - Not really. It's more about what he's into.

B - Oh absolutely! He loves to plea-sure me, too.

Is this consensual? Do you feel safe?

A - Honestly, I'm not always into it, and I

B - Always. We have a safe word, and

How is your communication?

B Incredible. We're very much on the same page.

A Not great. We struggle to listen to each other both in and out of the bedroom.

don't know how to tell him.

he always listens to me.

Do you like this person outside of the bedroom?

B Totally. Our relationship isn't just about sex.

A Not really, but the sex is so good.

Can you imagine having sex like this long term?

B Totally, I don't think I could go back now, TBH.

A It's fun for now, but I think about that a lot.

Mostly **A**

It doesn't sound like you're totally into it. You should feel like an equal not only in your relationship, but also in the bedroom. Try talking to your partner about your concerns and see if you can work through this.

Mostly **B**

Sounds like everything is working out. Keep up your excellent communication and remember to speak out if you don't feel comfortable.

Kink vs. Fetish

———

FETISH: **A sexual fixation on an act or an object that someone cannot be sexually satisfied without**

KINK: **More encompassing and includes a variety of sexual interests or fantasies (e.g., BDSM or role-playing)**

Types of Fetishes/Kinks:

Bondage:
Enjoying getting or being tied up

Cuckolding:
Arousal from the idea that your partner is sleeping with someone else

Dominance:
Pleasure from taking control in the bedroom

Electrostimulation:
Turned on by electric shock

Foot:
The most common; getting off by everything feet, from massaging and kissing feet to getting walked on or smelling dirty shoes

Gagging:
Enjoying watching your partner gag

Humiliation:
Pleasure in name-calling or verbal abuse

Impact Play:
Enjoying impact from hands, paddles, or whips

Lingerie:
A lot of people find this sexy, but when someone needs to see lingerie to get off, then it becomes a fetish.

Role-Playing:
Both partners pretending to be different ages or different characters to turn each other on (teacher/student, doctor/patient, etc.)

Sadomasochism:
Receiving or giving pleasure from pain or humiliation

Sensation Play:
Getting off from receiving or withholding different stimuli

Voyeurism:
Sexual pleasure from watching others naked or having sex

REMEMBER:
All fetishes are kinks, but not all kinks are fetishes.

Ask Someone Else

Guy I Dated: Andrew, 33, dated for about 1 month

The reason our date wasn't successful was just simply that we weren't a good match for each other. I don't think there's any hidden meaning or reasons behind it. I'm not really looking to drag up the past, and I'm fairly certain my girlfriend wouldn't be too happy about it, either.

Couple: Sabrina, 30, & Walker, 31, dating for about 9 months

Sabrina's partner has a cuckold fetish, so she wanted us to hook up and send him videos of our trysts. It was a blast, and it was such a turn-on knowing I was fulfilling not one, but two fantasies. I'm kind of an exhibitionist like that. The difference between a kink and a fetish, as I understand it, is that a kink is something that really turns you on, and a fetish is something you have a hard time getting off without. With any kink or fetish, the most important things are keeping an open mind and communicating. There is a lot of sexual shame and stigma out there, and it's easy to get caught up in that. If you're dating someone who confides in you about a kink they have, even if it's not your thing, remember that's a vulnerable place for them to be. So just by approaching with an open mind, you're already ahead of the pack. Now, that doesn't mean you owe them the fulfillment of this kink at all. Trust is key. As long as they bring it up respectfully, care about your consent (and your ability to withdraw consent if you're not into it), and you're somewhat interested, I'd say try it out! You might have more fun than you think.

Expert: Mistress Mina, dominatrix, @MistressMina

Foot fetishes are the most common fetish. I come across this all the time in my job, so I would embrace it. If you're dating someone with a foot fetish or any fetish, you have to talk about it. Think of the fetish as foreplay—it shouldn't be your entire sex life. I suggest 30 percent his fetish, and 70 percent your thing. Just make sure you communicate what you can put up with and what you can deal with.

16

THE GUY WHO'S NOT THAT INTO YOU

WON'T ASK YOU OUT

TAKES 3+ HOURS
TO TEXT YOU BACK

MET ONLINE

W hen I was little, the sight of facial hair sent me into hysterics. This was problematic, growing up in an Italian family in the late 1980s. As I grew, I stopped crying at the sight of face fuzz but still found beards gross because they were unknown: What was under there? Particles of food? What does his face really look like? Beards were pretty much a deal breaker for me, until I met Dean.

Dean had an extremely well-groomed beard. He was a *hunk of a man* with a gentlemanly vibe I thought had died with the Rat Pack. On our first date at a rooftop bar, he insisted I order a Negroni. Growing up Italian, I was familiar with this bitter cocktail, which I always thought tasted like cough syrup. But I couldn't say no to Dean's dark blue eyes. I took my first sip and liked it, and I started to like Dean, too.

After drinks, Dean asked if I wanted to check out this new trendy eatery in Hollywood. I was impressed by how he knew everyone who worked there. I suddenly understood his allure. After dinner, he took me to a cozy British gastropub for a nightcap. He told me this bar was like his home, and he rarely took dates there. I felt special. Then he kissed me.

The following weekend, he invited me to a poolside BBQ at his place. I brought pickles from my pickle guy at my local farmers' market, because when you live in LA for too long, you start acquiring connections like a "pickle guy." I was embarrassed to discover that despite his aesthetic, Dean didn't like pickles. Shouldn't this craft cocktail enthusiast also enjoy an artisanal pickle?

Later that night we celebrated our mutual Italian heritage at the Italian Festival. We expected a big band playing Sinatra and an endless selection of fine Italian food and flowing Chianti, and were disappointed with the sad red-checkered tablecloths, the one food vendor, and the location—it was a parking lot. We escaped to Dave and Buster's to pose in photo booths and play "pop a shot." Sure, it was a Sunday night, but with Dean, it was always a party.

Then I recognized we were rarely alone. Even at drinks and dinners, Dean was always chatting up the staff. I realized this was because he was a brand ambassador for a liquor company (naturally). Technically, he was on the clock every time we went on a date. But it didn't bother me. Dean was growing on me, and so was the bitter taste of Negronis.

TASTE:	LOOK:	SOUND:	SMELL:	FEEL:
Cilantro, and you're one of those people who taste cilantro as soap	Hotter than his photos	"That's Life" by Frank Sinatra	The great outdoors	Like an available cab just passed you by

One morning, I asked him the dreaded question. It had been a couple of months and many dates.

So I cooed, "Dean, what are we doing?"

"Uh . . . we're lying in bed," he said flatly.

"No, I mean this. What is this?"

Dean sighed loudly and stared at his three bikes mounted on this bedroom wall. Silence.

After what felt like an eternity, I had to ask, "So, what are you thinking?"

"I'm thinking I need to put air in those tires," he said curtly.

Dean couldn't have been clearer that he didn't want a girlfriend right now, but I hung on to "right now."

The more we dated, the more I noticed I was always initiating conversation. He'd always text me back; sometimes it would take hours, other times days. He never had an excuse, and he didn't owe me one.

On our last date, we went to see *Nocturnal Animals*—which, spoiler alert—ends with Jake Gyllenhaal ghosting on a date with Amy Adams. Not because he didn't like her, but because he was just indifferent. This was somewhat symbolic of our relationship. I stopped texting Dean after this date, and I never heard from him again.

The opposite of love is not hate, it's indifference. Dean obviously never loved me or hated me, but he was for sure indifferent. Then one girls' night I took a sip of my Negroni, and as the sugary bitter cocktail trickled down to the back of my throat, I realized I was indifferent towards Negronis, beards, and Dean. Why waste your time on a guy who's not that into you? You might be preventing yourself from meeting a guy who is.

Ways to Distract Yourself While You're Waiting for a Text Back

---

- ☐ KonMari your entire apartment.
- ☐ Do laundry.
- ☐ Write a musical.
- ☐ Make a detailed spreadsheet of all the guys you've hooked up with.
- ☐ Teach yourself how to cook something new!
- ☐ Read a book!
- ☐ Learn how to make your favorite cocktail!
- ☐ Delete any photos from your phone that are taking up too much space.
- ☐ Write a song.
- ☐ Attempt poetry.
- ☐ Call your mom!
- ☐ Call your friends!
- ☐ Watch *Friends,* since your real-life friends didn't pick up.
- ☐ Find all the tops to your food storage containers.
- ☐ Plan out all your outfits for the next week.

BOY BINGO

Takes him at least 3 hours to text you back	You're always making the plans 	Fun!
Always busy 	Free space! 	He's just not a great texter!
Different since you had sex	When you are together, he's distracted 	Future plans are met with "maybes"

IS HE JUST NOT THAT INTO YOU?

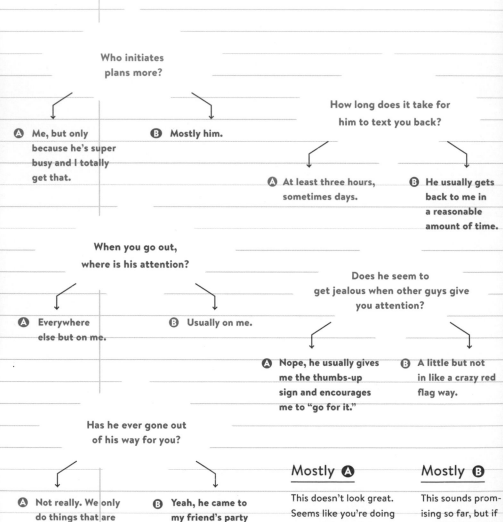

Who initiates plans more?

Ⓐ Me, but only because he's super busy and I totally get that.

Ⓑ Mostly him.

How long does it take for him to text you back?

Ⓐ At least three hours, sometimes days.

Ⓑ He usually gets back to me in a reasonable amount of time.

When you go out, where is his attention?

Ⓐ Everywhere else but on me.

Ⓑ Usually on me.

Does he seem to get jealous when other guys give you attention?

Ⓐ Nope, he usually gives me the thumbs-up sign and encourages me to "go for it."

Ⓑ A little but not in like a crazy red flag way.

Has he ever gone out of his way for you?

Ⓐ Not really. We only do things that are convenient for him, now that I think about it.

Ⓑ Yeah, he came to my friend's party the other night on the other side of town after a crazy long day at work.

Mostly Ⓐ

This doesn't look great. Seems like you're doing most of the work here, and a relationship should be a partnership, not one-sided. Try to have a conversation about how you're feeling and see if he hears you.

Mostly Ⓑ

This sounds promising so far, but if you're still unsure if he's into you, there's only one surefire way to find out: Ask him!

Ask Someone Else

Guy I Dated: Dean, 32, dated for 2 months

I think it's good. It's a weird thing to read, ya know? But I think you captured it well. The f*cking pickles. Haha. I forgot about that. I'm really trying to force myself to like them. Of course, that's really pretty much how it went. You could probably be way harsher about my detachment, etc. But I appreciate the generosity. I think girls probably recognize when there's not real compatibility long before guys do. Or maybe guys are just content to let it ride regardless. My advice would be to, maybe, just acknowledge it when you recognize it, and move on sooner rather than later?

Couple: Tina, 34, & Michael, 34, together 2½ years

We met online, but he didn't make a move after a month, so I thought he was gay. Fast-forward two years. We had dinner, and he made a move. I told him I should've married him, and I lost my chance. Less than two months later, we're engaged; seven months after that we're married. Now, two-and-a half-years in, we have a little girl and another baby on the way.

Expert: Andy Mizrahi, 31, most right-swiped guy on Tinder of 2018, @andymizrahi

I got notified in Spring 2018 that I had received 10,000 right swipes. But with matches, I'm a bit selective. I'm not one of those guys who just swipes and swipes and swipes. I actually (for some strange reason) look at profiles and swipe right on those who peak my interest, whether it's sexually or personality-wise. I'm more of a selective dude, and I like the in-person thing. Tinder to me was only for booty calls. I never treated it as serious dating. I texted back when the partner intrigued me, made it interesting, kept it sexy, and was maybe funny. Yes, I usually always respond to the funny ones. Okay, it's all about witty banter for me. If the girl has witty banter, I'm super down to keep talking.

17

THE GUY WHO'S GREAT ON PAPER

GREAT FOR SOMEONE ELSE!

PERFECT, BUT NO SPARK!

IT'S A MATCH!

m y mouth dropped when I saw the poster of Frank Sinatra's mugshot hanging in Brian's condo. "I thought you hated Sinatra." I couldn't help myself. "I do. But that's a dope photo." My Italian-American father would not approve.

Last night while texting, I admitted to Brian that Frank Sinatra's "Soliloquy" always pulls at my heartstrings. "Anyone who likes Sinatra only does because of their dad," he texted. I wanted to defend my love for Ol' Blue Eyes but sent an embarrassed emoji instead.

I let a lot slide with Brian. I was 29 and panicking that I hadn't met the right guy yet. After the devastating results of the 2016 election, I decided all you need is love. While my friends marched in protest, I marched to meet two matchmakers.

My matchmakers had me fill out a questionnaire where I divulged I was looking for a guy who was tall, funny, and smart, and wore glasses sometimes. Every few weeks I'd get drinks with a new match, and it would usually end there. Until I got introduced to Brian. On our first date over spicy margaritas, we told each other what we were looking for in a partner, and realized our descriptions perfectly captured each other. I was funny and

blondish, and he wore glasses sometimes! I quickly felt the chemistry. I mean, *of course* we had chemistry. We were a perfect match!

After our date, we texted nonstop, bonding over the ridiculousness of Martin Scorsese's Instagram (for a world-class director, he really posts a lot of backlit photos). Brian asked me out on a second date that Friday night. The plan was to meet at his place for drinks and then go to dinner at a French bistro.

I was in awe of how meticulously decorated his place was. Then I noticed the five pie stands. "So, you're really into pie?" I asked. He didn't get it. "Why do you have multiple pie stands?" "Oh, my mom decorated." Then I saw the potpourri, multiple candles, and throw pillows. All touches a 30-year-old straight man would not make without some persistent female energy. He handed me a glass of what he referred to as "smoky tequila" (mezcal) over ice with Snapple Diet Peach Tea. I sipped it, trying not to make a face.

At dinner, he asked hard-hitting questions, covering everything from my relationship with my mother to my abusive ex. When I questioned him about his damage, he said, "My life has been pretty

TASTE:	LOOK:	SOUND:	SMELL:	FEEL:
Vegan gluten-free pizza	What you say you want in a guy, but you're actually not attracted to	"Everything You Want" by Vertical Horizon	Opening a brand-new textbook	Shower sex

great so far." He asked why I was barely touching my food. On the theme of honesty, I admitted the veal was tough and the risotto tasted like chlorine.

We went back to his place and over another round of Snapple and mezcal, we took turns playing our favorite songs. He called my choice of "Africa" by Toto "too basic" as he put on "Chateau Lobby #4 (in C for Two Virgins)" by Father John Misty. When the lyric "and I haven't left your bed since" hit, he kissed me, and my judgment toward Brian melted away like the ice in my cocktail.

The next morning in my Uber home, I upgraded him in my phone from "Maybe Brian" to "Brian." I was pretty sure I'd hear from him later, but I didn't. It was weird. We used to text every day. I gave it time.

Nine p.m. on Monday was all the time I could handle. I texted him, "Great news! Finally got home from my Uber!" We joked about my fake kidnapping. Then I saw the three gray dots.

Typing.

Typing.

Typing.

Finally, after what felt like a year, "Gabi I don't know what to do. . . . If I'm being honest, I'm not sure if our relationship has long-term potential. I'm at that age where I'm saying, 'Is this my wife?' after every date. I'd like to keep hanging out, but I also am not sure how serious it would be. . . ."

Then it hit me. *I* didn't see long term in this relationship. This was not *my* husband. How I would I even begin to explain to my dad that Brian thought the *Chairman of the Board* was "overrated." Also, the pie holders. *Why did he have so many pie holders?* That was insane. It didn't matter if on paper we were the perfect match; in person, we were just not compatible.

BOY BINGO

Astrologically compatible	**You were set up**	**Exactly what you tell people you want in a partner**
Matched on every dating app	**Free space!** 	**Maybe better as friends?**
Vanilla sex	**Wouldn't have given him the time of day in high school or college**	**You *really* want to like him**

Your Dating Resume

You're also really great on paper! To remind yourself, make a dating résumé. (Here's mine for an example.) This a fun thing to do while you're waiting for a text back. Don't show potential dates. Or do. Do you!

NAME

Gabi Conti

OBJECTIVE

To find love in a hopeless place. A partner in crime, an equal, someone who loves me the way I am but also challenges me.

1. EXPERIENCE

Guy Who Was My Person
2017–2018

Lived with this 33-year-old man-child, where I mastered the art of couples costumes and tolerating video games. Well versed in all the *Mission: Impossible* movies, and developed a new appreciation for Tom Cruise. (He does all his own stunts! THAT'S INSANE!)

2. SKILLS

Proficient in AIM, Facebook Messenger, Gchat, sliding into DMs, texting, drunk texting but not seeming drunk at all, drunk dialing, selfies, Skype, WhatsApp, and FaceTime. Can speak conversational Bro, Geek, Vegan, and Hipster. 420 friendly. Excellent chef, motivational speaker, interior designer, and arm candy. Great with parents, dogs, and cats!

3. EDUCATION

Camp Vega for Girls
1997–2002

Learned crucial life skills, like how to straighten my hair, shave my legs, and flirt with the boys' camp without looking desperate.

Alpha Epsilon Phi
2005–2009

Mastered chugging an entire bottle of cheap champagne, learned how to throw a theme party, honed the ability to care about things I really don't care about!

Guy Who Was Younger than Me
2016

Developed the appreciation and respect for pregaming.

Guy Who Was Not My Boyfriend
2015

Discovered six months is for sure the longest I could date someone I really care about without a title.

Guy Who Was Cooler than Me
2011–2012

Learned to appreciate house music, nightclubs, and watching football. Honed my ability to decode drunk texts. Managed the whereabouts of his wallet, keys, and cellphone. Coordinated airport pickups and drop-offs.

Guy Who Was Older than Me
2010–2011

Developed a high tolerance for *60 Minutes*, long dinners, and classical music. Can hold my own with people significantly older than me.

SHOULD YOU DATE THE GUY WHO'S GREAT ON PAPER?

Are you at all attracted to him?

Ⓐ Not really.

Ⓑ Yeah, there's definitely a spark. Not fireworks, but a spark for sure.

How are your conversations?

Ⓐ Feels like pulling teeth.

Ⓑ So funny! We can't stop texting. He really cracks me up.

How compatible are your tastes in music, food, movies, TV shows, etc.?

Ⓐ We can't seem to agree on any of those things.

Ⓑ Pretty compatible. I mean I don't agree with him on everything, but we have enough common ground.

Can you picture yourself having sex with him?

Ⓐ Gross.

Ⓑ Actually yeah, I bet he'd be good.

When you're hanging out, who calls the shots on what you're doing?

Ⓐ Always him. He shuts down most of my ideas.

Ⓑ It's pretty equal!

Mostly Ⓐ

This guy might be great on paper, but he doesn't seem too impressive in practice (or person). There seem to be challenges with you two connecting. Give it time if it seems worth it, and let the relationship develop naturally.

Mostly Ⓑ

There's a lot of potential here. Seems like you're in your head about whether or not you should date this guy. Give it time and see what develops!

Ask Someone Else

Guy I Dated: Brian, 32, went on 2 dates

I thought you were funny, interesting, and easy to talk to. I know if a guy breaks up with you after you have sex, the logical conclusion is, "He's an asshole who just wanted sex and now that he got it, he's moving on." I've heard women say this a lot, and it always kind of bugs me because it implies that there is no universe where a dude could've simply not enjoyed a sexual experience. I think men should be just as entitled as women to end things after feeling like there's no chemistry (physical or emotional). There have been plenty of times where I would start hooking up with a girl and recognize that this was not a relationship I was interested in pursuing but felt obligated to continue dating her just so she didn't feel used. As I've grown older and had more experiences, I've come to terms with the fact that it's better ending things as soon I realize that this is not a relationship I

want to be in. I'm sure it was hurtful for you at the moment, but ultimately, it seems like it was the right move for us both. And I'm sorry I gave you Snapple, own pie holders, and don't care for old music. I am working on myself!

Experts: Lauren Rosenberg & Jaydi Samuels, LJMatchmaking, my matchmakers

Hate that we played a part in that experience, but it's a perfect example of how sometimes men or women present themselves to us one way but are totally different in a dating scenario. And it's not malicious. They simply have some realizations "in the field" that they didn't have when being "interviewed." I guess that's why it's more of an art than a science. If it were a science, boy, would our jobs be easy! Still a bummer, though, as we were so excited about that particular match. Onto the next one!

Another Expert: Annabel Gat, astrologer, author of *The Astrology of Love & Sex*

Sun sign compatibility is such an insightful and fun way to learn more about yourself and relationship dynamics, but the truth is that astrology can take someone only so far. Any Aries can be an angel or an asshole. It's really up to the person to be ready for a relationship, and compatibility or astrology can't tell you that. There is no prescribed perfect person for you based on your birth chart. But astrology is a fantastic tool to get to know yourself. And when you know yourself, everything else, like relationships, is much easier! Astrology can give us tools and ways to better understand each other and communicate, which is the bedrock of all relationships. Sometimes the signs that are said to be the least compatible end up forming the most life-changing relationships.

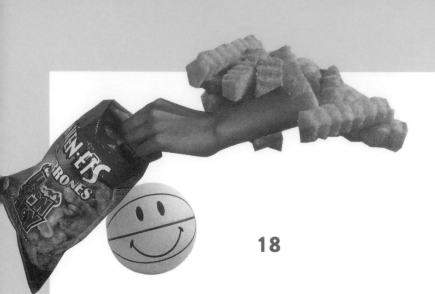

18

THE GUY WHO'S MUCH YOUNGER

I DON'T KNOW ABOUT YOU,
BUT I'M FEELING 22!
(JK I'M 29 AND THIS
IS CREEPY)

it was Valentine's Day. I was 29 and my date, Leo, was 22. We kept reminding each other that despite the Hallmark holiday, this date wasn't anything special. The plan was to grab happy hour sushi and see a movie. Since Leo had just graduated college, he insisted we pregame first. College pre-gaming usually involves crushing beers and downing shots. You do this because you're too young to drink in public and/or it's so much cheaper. Leo knew I was far from college, so he kept it classy by bringing over not one, but two bottles of white wine, and encouraged me to "chug" before we headed to the movie.

I had met Leo at a historic three-story bar in downtown Los Angeles a couple of weeks prior. We were waiting in line for a speakeasy tiki bar when Leo and I locked eyes. Probably because I was in heels, we literally saw eye to eye. Leo looked like a lanky Hemsworth: blond, dark eyebrows, and just the right amount of intentional scruff. When I first found out he was seven years my junior, I didn't mind—probably because I was fresh off a juice cleanse and on my third Vodka Soda (vodka's basically potato juice, right?).

Leo also felt older than 22. When we finally got into the tiki bar, he offered to buy me a drink. He got my number and made plans to see me again. Then he followed up on those plans. He really wanted to take me on a picnic under the stars at the Griffith Observatory. I was impressed. Most of the guys I went on dates with would half-heartedly suggest we grab a drink at a bar walking distance to their apartment.

We kept dating, and as much as I enjoyed Leo's company, Googling "celebrity couples where the woman is older," and playing Taylor Swift's "22" on a loop, deep down I knew our age gap would soon tear us apart.

Then one morning we ran into one of Leo's friends at a coffee shop. "Bro! Last night was so f*ckin' lit! You really missed out!" This "bro" exclaimed at a volume of someone still drunk from the night before. I almost spit out my pour-over coffee. Then I saw the FOMO in Leo's eyes. He really did miss out.

On the walk back to my place, I was distracted by how handsomely disheveled Leo looked in the mid-morning sun. Until he started doing an impression of Cartman from *South Park*. It hit me that his sense of humor was essentially impressions. This was also my sense of humor at 22. My best friend, Ayler, and I did Borat impressions until people would have to literally beg us to stop.

TASTE:	LOOK:	SOUND:	SMELL:	FEEL:
Red Bull	Fratty Bro	Bad impressions	Lysol	Like Mrs. Robinson

After that morning, we kept making and breaking plans. Finally, our sunset Griffith Observatory picnic date came up, and we both agreed to cancel at the last minute. For me, the idea of sitting in the dirt felt unappealing. As for Leo, I'm assuming he preferred to have a "lit" night with bros closer to his age. Now he pops up on Instagram looking happy with a girlfriend who's more age appropriate. I'd like to think I helped Leo grow up a little, and he helped remind me of an important college lesson: You can save a ton of money on alcohol when you pregame.

BOYS vs. MEN

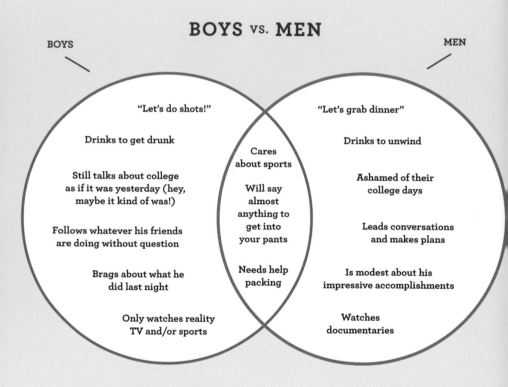

BOYS

"Let's do shots!"

Drinks to get drunk

Still talks about college as if it was yesterday (hey, maybe it kind of was!)

Follows whatever his friends are doing without question

Brags about what he did last night

Only watches reality TV and/or sports

Cares about sports

Will say almost anything to get into your pants

Needs help packing

MEN

"Let's grab dinner"

Drinks to unwind

Ashamed of their college days

Leads conversations and makes plans

Is modest about his impressive accomplishments

Watches documentaries

BOY BINGO

Can turn almost anything into a drinking game	**Has more energy than you**	**The only married couple he knows is his parents**
Finds night clubs fun and exciting!	**Free space!** 	**Recently graduated from college**
Has at least two roommates	**Has one-night stands, but no nightstands**	**Loves video games**

Quiz

IS HE TOO YOUNG FOR YOU?

What does his apartment look like?

Ⓐ Clothes everywhere, dirty toilet. I've seen cleaner frat houses, TBH.

Ⓑ Clean! He has a maid come in once a month and cleans in between.

What's in his fridge?

Ⓐ Beer mostly. And is that Lunchables?

Ⓑ Fresh farmers' market produce and all the essentials to make breakfast in the morning.

How much younger is he?

Ⓐ More than five years.

Ⓑ Less than five years.

How do you fight?

Ⓐ He usually ignores me after I confront him about something.

Ⓑ We have frank and honest discussions.

What is his perfect Saturday night?

Ⓐ Going to a house party or a club and getting wasted with his bros.

Ⓑ A bottle of wine, a delicious dinner, and maybe a movie.

Mostly Ⓐ

Sounds like he still has some growing up to do. You want to feel like an equal in your relationship and not your guy's mother and or maid.

Mostly Ⓑ

This guy really seems to have his life together. Lock him down!

Ask Someone Else

Guy I Dated: Leo, 23, dated for 1 month

One thing I'll say to defend myself (and my sense of humor) is that I probably realized my FOMO was conspicuous and got embarrassed. I tended to deflect my awkward nervousness with impressions. Guess it's easier pretending to be someone else when you're still in the awkward stages of figuring yourself out.

Couple: Carly, 35, & Patrick, 27, together for 4 years

For a long time, we were very self-conscious about what other people would think of us. Now we DGAF (don't give a f*ck). Let him reach maturity milestones on his own. You're not his mom or his life coach. Embrace the different stages you are both in naturally in your own lives, internally and externally. Focus on the qualities that attracted you to each other in the first place, and stay in the present.

Expert: Victoria, 33, exclusively dates younger men

Every boyfriend I've had has been younger than me. The gap is as little as one year and as large as seven years. The age difference was an issue for me with my first super-serious boyfriend, who was 20 when I was 25. He eventually turned 21, so we were only four years apart for a few months, but I felt guilty dating someone who wasn't even old enough to drink. He was so sweet and so committed to pursuing me. We never discussed the age difference, and people always thought he was older than me. The one big issue that later affected our relationship was the fact that we were going in different directions in life (I was in law school and he was an actor). He also wasn't much of a reader and often didn't understand my cultural or literary references. Don't mistake intimacy for communication. Younger guys are sweet and tend to be more affectionate, but like all males, they suffer from an acute inability to actually hear and understand what you're saying. Give him a little leeway when it comes to understanding you and your priorities, but don't forget to clearly communicate what you want. At the end of the day, love is love. If two people decide to work on a relationship so it flourishes, that's what's going to determine its lasting power.

19

THE GUY WHO MAKES YOU DO YOU

IT'S TIME TO
BREAK THOSE
PATTERNS, BABY!

1 was standing on a chair taking an overhead shot of this hunk of "La Lasagna Land" I made for the Oscar viewing party I was hosting. And I know this sounds ridiculous, but it was 2017, and that's just how we took pictures of food!

My two friends, Jenna and Perry, used the flashlight on their phones so we could perfectly light this lasagna. Perry asked me who this photo was for, and I told her about Dan. We'd gone on our first date two nights prior, and there were fireworks. We saw *La La Land* and loved it. Even though Dan and I only knew each other for three days, we were already yellow heart, three fire sign emoji status on Snapchat. Which meant that we were each other's best friend and on a three-day Snapchat streak. So much of our relationship was measured in views, likes, and text backs. But he's "kind of an asshole," I confessed to my friends as I snapped the photo.

Regardless, I was pretty positive Dan was my soulmate. Not only did Dan look just like my type: tall, blond, with a slight Patrick Bateman "Will he kill me? Let's find out" vibe. We both had a photo of us doing yoga in Thailand around the same time. Meant to be, right? Or, it just meant we were two white people doing "yoga" in Thailand seeking validation through likes on Instagram.

So on our second date, when Dan asked if I wanted to go on an overnight wine tasting trip with him to Santa Barbara, I said yes, even though my friends were convinced he was going to murder me.

So, the first thing we did in Santa Barbara was take a picture at Fisherman's Wharf that looked like Dan was pushing me off the dock to send to all my concerned friends. He handed me back my phone and asked me if I knew my pictures were live. That's a setting that lets you hear and see what was happening when your photos were being taken. He held up the picture of lasagna, with my voice slurring, "He's kinda an asshole." "Who were you talking about?" he demanded. "Uh . . . definitely not you," I lied. We shook it off with sunset cocktails. And I started to notice we were both Snapchatting this trip. I was putting everything up for everyone to see, but when I looked at his Snapchat, there was nothing.

TASTE:	LOOK:	SOUND:	SMELL:	FEEL:
Burnt marshmallows	If he was in a lineup with your exes, you'd have a hard time picking him out	"Blank Space" by Taylor Swift	Clean laundry	Obsessed

Back in the inn, I asked him why. He blew up, "I'm not your boyfriend. I don't need to tell you anything. We're over. Let's go." And he started to pack up his duffle bag.

See, that's the problem with having a type. You're dating the same person over and over again and not growing or learning from your mistakes. As he yelled at me, I saw all my other relationships that started great but came crashing down. How did I miss the red flags, again?

The next morning was like nothing had ever happened. We went wine tasting, where we met a married couple who thought we were married. We both posted videos of us feeding these ostriches we met on the ride back to LA.

On the trip back, I asked him what his favorite part of our adventure was. He said he didn't know and asked me. I told him how much fun it was wine tasting and feeding the ostriches with him, and how funny it was when that couple thought we were married when technically it was only our fourth date.

He looked at me like I had just told him I actually hated *La La Land* and snapped, "See, Gabi, this is why you'll never be happy. All of your happiness is reliant on other people. This is over. We're done."

I guess sometimes it takes a guy who isn't your boyfriend to dump you not once, but twice to make you realize you need to break your dating patterns and focus on yourself. Also, if you're in a fresh, new, exciting relationship, and it seems too good to be true, be careful! And make sure your iPhone photos aren't live!

How to Date Yourself

☐ Realize and recognize it's time to focus on yourself.

☐ Make yourself a set of goals that depict what dating yourself looks like. Does this mean not going on dates? Does this mean taking time before you call someone your boyfriend? Are there certain red flags or nonnegotiables you are going to avoid?

☐ Talk to your friends and family about your plan and have them hold you accountable.

☐ If you can afford it, try to consult with a therapist or a life coach. If you can't, look into self-help books.

☐ Practice self-care, whatever that means to you. Maybe that's working out more, doing yoga, taking time to be by yourself, cutting out foods and drinks that make you feel gross after, reading a book, or pampering yourself.

☐ Distance yourself from any toxic people who make you doubt your self-worth, or guys can't give you what you want.

☐ Once you have finally made yourself a priority and feel ready to get back out there, do it. But still be aware of your patterns, and keep putting yourself first until someone proves worthy of being your partner.

BOY BINGO

You're trying to recreate memories from past relationships with him	You're ignoring obvious red flags	Déjà vu
It's moving too fast	Free space! 	You don't trust him
Something's off, but can't put your finger on it	He's kind of an asshole	He's always blowing up your phone *DING! DING! DING!*

Quiz

IS IT TIME TO BREAK THOSE PATTERNS?

Will a boyfriend solve all your problems?

Ⓐ Yeah. It's called happily ever after because your problems are over!

Ⓑ No. Only I can solve my problems.

Did you learn and heal from your last relationship?

Ⓐ Working on it, but you know what they say: The best way to get over someone is to get under someone else!

Ⓑ Yes, I am constantly growing, learning, and evolving.

Do you love yourself?

Ⓐ Not really. But that's what dating's for, right? To find someone to love me, so I can finally love myself!

Ⓑ I'm not perfect, but I accept myself for who I am, and I am always working on improving myself.

Think about your last few relationships. Do you notice any patterns in terms of issues or red flags?

Ⓐ Yeah . . .

Ⓑ Not really. Each relationship was different.

Do you believe in finding your "other half"?

Ⓐ Yep! And I know he's out there. I just haven't met him yet.

Ⓑ No. I'm a whole person, and when I'm ready I'll meet another whole person. Together we will complement each other and form an equal and loving partnership.

Mostly Ⓐ

It's time to break those patterns, Baby. Work on you. Here are some things that might help: therapy, new hobbies, surrounding yourself with supportive people, learning new things about yourself. Make *you* super strong, and then you'll be ready to get back out there.

Mostly Ⓑ

Sounds like you broke those patterns. Go you! Of course, relationships are work, too, but you sound like you really worked on yourself.

Ask Someone Else

Guy I Dated: Dan, 33, dated for 1 (very intense) week

Oh boy. I like it [the story]. Read it twice. Definitely laughed, definitely pondered, definitely felt like an asshole. We moved quickly. I pushed back. Became critical, which was really just projecting. I actually recognized that a lot of my nature and desire to help others "improve" was a reflection of my own need to improve myself. Sorry to have ever made you feel bad about who you are; I thought/think you're a great woman.

Me: Gabi

I wish I could tell you that after I dated Dan, I quit dating for a while, focused on myself, and made sure I never repeated these patterns again—but actually, I started talking to Neal (next chapter) around the same time. There were a lot of red flags with Neal that I ignored because I was so swept up in the romance. I wonder if I would have broken my patterns if I'd paused after Dan, and didn't allow myself to get into a relationship. Now I'm not allowing myself to call anyone my boyfriend for at least a couple of months, and already it feels like it's working. I think my biggest takeaway from all this is to remember that being alone isn't scary—it's empowering. Embrace it and don't dwell on the loneliness, because you can feel just as lonely in a relationship, especially a bad one.

Expert: Megan Bruneau, MA therapist, executive coach, writer, and speaker who's dated the f*ck outta Manhattan

It's *always* time to focus on you, so perhaps the moment you notice you're not focusing on yourself, you know it's time to focus on you. Whether we're in a relationship or not, many of us consciously or unconsciously believe that our worth is dependent on serving someone else's needs. As a result, we end up sacrificing our own needs and well-being and end up resentful, depressed, anxious, and lonely, despite being in a relationship.

The first step is awareness; we can't change what we aren't aware of! And with that, something called "self-compassion" is a game changer for liking yourself and life a little more.

If you can afford it, get therapy or coaching with someone who specializes in attachment patterns. If you can't afford a therapist, I recommend reading up on attachment styles, journaling, and reflecting on identifying patterns you want to change.

I also recommend yoga or another form of meditation to help learn how to be with discomfort, because dating is super uncomfortable, and when we react to that discomfort through avoidance, then we fall back into the same unconscious habits/patterns.

20

THE GUY WHO'S YOUR PERSON

IS THIS IT?

AT LAST/END GAME

HAPPILY EVER

AFTER . . . FOR NOW

"my parents are moving out of my childhood home," I stammered through tears over dirty martinis. "Is that why you brought me here?!" Neal looked annoyed. We were at the country club in my hometown. On the green, a couple was getting married. Marriage used to feel within reach for us. I couldn't believe my partner of almost two years could be this insensitive. If he can't sympathize with this change that affected my parents more than me, more than *us*, how could we get through the other changes in our future?

Neal and I had a slow burn into love. It started over drinks. Everyone around us assumed we were dating, and it wasn't even a date. Over vodka sodas, I found myself attracted to Neal's preppy style, cleft chin, and goofy demeanor. The more we hung out, the more he romanticized all our relationship milestones. First, on a shared iPhone note with a To Do list including everything from "brunch" to "parents' house." Then, in a photo album with snapshots of us posing in photo booths holding up signs like "We should make out," to us standing by the tent we pitched after driving from LA to Oregon to see the 2017 total eclipse. We built a Spotify playlist soundtracking our courtship. "Hold on to the memories, I will hold on to you" from Taylor Swift's "New Year's Day" summed up our love.

We held on to each other as we both lost our jobs in LA. Then he got a job in New York and asked if I wanted to move to Brooklyn with him. "We are just two kids in love and this feels like our home," he told the real estate agent when we found our place in East Williamsburg. We knew the L train (our access to Manhattan) would shut down in a couple of months. It didn't matter. Our love would prevail!

He was already in Brooklyn when I packed up my life in LA. My friends came over in shifts to help. Breaking apart Ikea furniture, sorting through nine years of dresses, throwing away old drafts of scripts and headshots. All the things that kept me grounded over the past nine years in Hollywood were gone in a couple of days. At 30, for the first time in my life, I put love instead of my career first.

The first couple of months in Brooklyn I felt lucky waking up every morning next to Neal. Then I noticed I was more alone in this relationship than when I was single. I'd moved here to be with Neal, and most nights he wouldn't come home until 2 a.m. At first, because he was working late, then to host a video game show. Now well, I guess I'll never know.

TASTE:	LOOK:	SOUND:	SMELL:	FEEL:
Chicken noodle soup	Cute in a couple's costume	The crackling of a fireplace	Eggs and bacon sizzling in the morning	A big warm hug

When he was home, it felt like he wasn't there, glassy-eyed and lost in a video game world, having one-word conversations. "I feel like you don't support me," I cried to him one night. "I pay rent, don't I?!" he barked back.

The following weekend we were at my parents' house. "We're getting tacos?! I don't eat tacos on the East Coast!" he snapped when I told him our dinner plans. My parents noticed how moody and rude he was acting. They couldn't understand what I saw in him, and at the time neither could I. It was around then that I started to mourn "us."

I cried into my mother's arms. She asked me if I remembered her first marriage. Boy, did I ever. Especially since I learned about it only a couple of years ago. Sure, I was always suspicious that my tiny larger-than-life mother didn't have a wedding to fit her personality. I always pictured my mom with a team of bridesmaids, a four-hundred-person guest list, a reception in a five-star hotel or restaurant, a full orchestra playing as she walked down the aisle, and of course, a big, white Vera Wang gown.

When actually, it was the opposite. My mother got married to my father in a small church. She wore a vintage satin cream skirt suit (I should've known, cream is *such* a second-wedding color). There were no bridesmaids.

When I asked my dad what their wedding song was for their thirty-nine years of marital bliss, he sent me a YouTube link to "popular love songs in the 70s" and encouraged me to "pick one." Which is insane. Thirty-nine years of marriage and you don't have a song?! I have songs with guys I've dated for thirty-nine minutes.

When I was 27 my mom finally told me about Derek, a man she used to think was her person, like I thought Neal was mine. She met him when she was a flight attendant for American Airlines in the early 1970s, on a red-eye from JFK to LAX. Derek was a first-class passenger from California with blue eyes and blond hair. This was impressive to my mother from Brooklyn, back when living in Brooklyn wasn't something you bragged about.

It was love at first "Peanuts?" and they stayed up the whole flight chatting. He was "from money, but worked in leather," which apparently was a socially acceptable career choice in the 1970s. My mom and Derek had been dating for only five weeks when he asked her to marry him. They had the wedding I always imagined my Bridezilla mother having. She wore a big, white dress, they got married at a beautiful church, and they had a reception at Tavern on the Green, where they danced to their song, "Moon River" from *Breakfast at Tiffany's*.

After the wedding, they lived in New York, and he cheated on her. So they moved to Provincetown, where he cheated on her again but promised to be better. And then she walked in on him having a threesome with a couple. So my tiny mom got a moving van and moved back in with her mom in Brooklyn.

Two months after I realized Neal and I didn't have a future, I also moved back in with my parents. While he didn't cheat on me like Derek did with my mom (at least to my knowledge), I felt emotionally cheated. Like the time I turned 31 and cried about getting older and not feeling accomplished. Neal refused to hug me because I was "being dramatic." Or the time I realized I gave up my career in Los Angeles to be with him in Brooklyn, and he snapped, "Like things were really working out for you in Hollywood!" Or anytime I'd tell him I was going to go onstage and he'd warn me I better go over it with him first because the last time "wasn't that great." This was not the man I fell in love with.

At first, it felt like my life was over, being 31, single, and living with my parents. Then I realized my life was actually beginning. Just like my mom's life began again when she left Derek. Being 24, single, and living with your parents in the 1970s had the same shame associated with being 31, single, and living with your parents today. But soon my mom got her own place and started working in advertising, where she met my dad, her real person, who she married when she was 30. And while they didn't have a big wedding, now they have a strong marriage. Almost forty years of love spent standing by each other's side no matter what. When my mom got sick with cancer, my dad (pre-Internet) went to our local library every day until he tracked down the one doctor who could cure her. And now my mom is over twenty years cancer free. If I ever got sick, I can't imagine Neal doing the same for me.

Sure, my parents didn't find each other until later in their lives, but look how happy they are. Isn't true love worth the wait? Given the choice, I'd choose a strong marriage over a big wedding any day. So if you don't find your person in your twenties, don't freak out. Being in your thirties and single isn't that bad. As for my person? Well, perhaps I just haven't met him yet.

LIKE vs. LUST vs. LOVE

LIKE

LUST

"He's fine."

"He's perfect!"

"I should probably look cute for date night, but I'm not going to drive myself crazy."

"I would literally die if he saw me in sweats."

Still getting to know each other

"We talk a little; still getting to know him."

"We have to have sex every time we hang out or else!"

"I know a lot about him, but there are still some blank spaces."

"Sure, I'd have sex with him."

"There's nothing really to fight about yet."

Out of the friend zone

"It's funny, we actually never fight!"

Chill

Passion!

"He's not perfect, but I still love him."

"He likes me the best in sweats without makeup. I know he's full of it, but it's still sweet."

"We have sex when we have sex. I'm not worried about our sex life."

"We could talk about literally anything."

LOVE

"Our fights make us stronger."

137

IS HE YOUR PERSON?

Would you be cool
having sex with just him for the
rest of your life?

Ⓐ Um . . .

Ⓑ Duh!

Could you see having
a family with him? Do you think
he'd make a good dad?

Ⓐ He still has some
growing up to do.

Ⓑ Totally!

Do you want similar
things out of life?

Ⓐ Not really.

Ⓑ Yep. We have
compatible
futures.

Do your family and
friends like him?

Ⓐ Not really.

Ⓑ Adore him!

If you got really sick,
what would he do?

Ⓐ He might
leave me.

Ⓑ Stay by my side
and help me get
better.

Mostly Ⓐ

Sounds like he still has
some growing up to do.
Not saying dump him,
just be aware of these
issues and make sure
you talk about what's
bothering you.

Mostly Ⓑ

Sounds like you
met your match!

BOY BINGO

You really see a life with him	You are equals	Help each other through problems both big and small
Have excellent communication	**Free space!**	**Love and accept each other**

You trust each other	**Plans for the future align**	**Wherever you're together = home**
	The Future NEXT EXIT	

Ask Somebody Else

Guy I Dated: Neal, 33, together 2 years

Our story is a lot more than this, but I've taken away two things: absolute honesty and consistent dependability. In relationships, you have to be brutally honest with yourself and your partner. They are your partner! Your best friend! Never be scared to hurt your partner with the truth. You also have to be consistent.

After the breakup, I watched the *BoJack Horseman* episode "Free Churro" almost every day for a month (seriously, Netflix can check this data). I think this quote from that episode, written by creator Raphael Bob-Waksberg, says it best: "In TV, flawed characters are constantly showing people they care with these surprising grand gestures. And I think that part of me still believes that's what love is. But in real life, the big gesture isn't enough. You need to be consistent, you need to be dependably good . . . You need to do it every day, which is so . . . hard."

Or in our situation: You can't just screw everything up and make an iMovie slideshow of your relationship set to Taylor Swift's "New Year's Day."

My Parents: Paul & Julie Conti, together 39 years

I knew as soon as we first met and looked into each other's eyes. We both knew this was something. We laugh a lot. We see the humor in everything. We hug each other every day. Also, can you take out the part where it says I'm from Brooklyn? —Julie

Your mother's grandmother told her a couple should never go to bed angry at each other. Always make up before you go to bed. When you find the right person, you just feel it inside. There's something inside your heart and your head that says this is the person I want to be with. And I found that with your mother. Celebrate all the important anniversaries. I remember walking through her neighborhood in Brooklyn and feeling very homey, like this was

someone I could build a life with. —Paul

Couple: Ali, 35 & Matt, 36, together 8 months

I met my guy off Bumble after many failed attempts and bad dates. I had just had my heart broken again and was out of town photographing a wedding. I decided I needed to go home to see my best friend before heading back to Portland. Because of that decision, I had to drive home a different way than normal, and it took me outside of the usual radius I had set on Bumble. We matched right away. Timing is everything, and if I hadn't made the last-minute decision to go see her instead of coming home immediately, I may never have matched with him. Here we are eight months later, and we already know that marriage and a lifetime together is happening for us.

NOW WHAT?

When I was writing this book, I went from thinking I found my happily ever after at 29, to single and living with my parents at 31, to living on my own for the first time in a studio apartment in Hollywood. It's been a roller coaster, but worth every lesson and tear.

Here's what I figured out writing this and interviewing exes, couples, and experts. There is one constant link between why relationships work or fail, and that's communication. This seems so basic, right? You also might think you're already communicating, but are you really listening? I know I sure wasn't. For example, when The Guy Who Wasn't That Into Me said he didn't want "a girlfriend right now," I just heard "right now."

Sometimes we only hear what we want to hear when we're dating. Or we're so terrified about losing a person and being (gasp!) alone that we don't say what we need to say. Don't do what I did and not realize this until you're 31, living in Brooklyn with a boyfriend who makes you feel more alone than you've ever felt in your entire life.

I was also shocked by how many exes wanted to chat after all this time had passed. I had the excuse of writing this book, but I think (after enough time has passed) there's nothing wrong with talking to your ex. It's easier than ever to track them down these days! You really can learn a lot from past relationships. You might even discover The Guy Who Ghosts didn't mean to ghost, or the Guy Who's Not Your Boyfriend really wanted to be your boyfriend and wasn't seeing other women, he was just scared, or the Guy Who Texts You "sup" at 2 a.m. had no idea you liked him more than a booty call. Life is too short to not really say what's in your heart and on your mind. And that's the other common theme with successful relationships: honesty. You can get over any of these obstacles in dating, as long as you and your partner are honest with each other.

As for dating in my thirties, so far it has been *SO* much fun. It is such a thrill to be older and wiser, know what I want, not play games, and not hang on to a maybe. I can't wait to tell you more, but I guess you'll just have to wait for *Thirty Guys You Date in Your Thirties* . . .

HEY, THANKS!

I'd like to thank my hairstylists, Paul Jean and Fabion at Paul Jean Salon, who not only never let me get bangs during my many breakups, but also introduced me to my now lit manager, David Styne. David believed in this book when it was just two chapters, and got it to Chris George, who got it to my now book agent Beth Davey, at Davey Literary & Media, who got it to Zaneta Jung at Chronicle, who really helped develop this book into what you just read. You would not be reading this book without this phenomenal team that I am forever grateful for. And big thanks to my lawyer, Marios Rush, for making sure none of my exes sue me. I also have to thank my storytelling coach, David Crabb, who helped me shape these stories from sometimes angsty diary entries into (hopefully) relatable experiences. Thank you to all the guys I wrote about who were so cool and supportive about this book. I'd also like to thank my therapist and friend, John Kim, for keeping me sane between breakups, and my friends throughout my life for always keeping me grounded. Especially my best friend since high school, Emily Hardin, who has met almost every ex and has been my guiding light through dating in my twenties. And my ride or die Amy Cheapho, who gave me a couch to crash on when I moved back to LA and the truth I needed to hear. Thank you to my dear friend Stephen Christy for his unwavering honesty and support during this book-writing process. Thank you to Nikki Glaser, Anthony Jeselnik, Demetri Martin, Gaby Dunn, Shawn Binder, Lindsey Rosin, Martie Cook, and Kevin S. Bright for saying nice things about me in my proposal that I'm assuming helped Chronicle trust me to write a whole book. I also have to thank my parents again, as I'm an only child and I'm sure dedicating this book to them is not enough, because nothing ever is!